Drugs and Development

Opium poppy cultivation in Laos.

Drugs and Development

The Global Impact on Sustainable Growth and Human Rights

Merrill Singer
University of Connecticut

WAVELAND

PRESS, INC.

Long Grove, Illinois

For information about this book, contact:
  Waveland Press, Inc.
  4180 IL Route 83, Suite 101
  Long Grove, IL 60047-9580
  (847) 634-0081
  info@waveland.com
  www.waveland.com

Cover: Photo by R. C. Matharaj (Dreamstime)
Frontispiece and photos on pages 1, 13, 19, 21, 61, and 68 courtesy of
the United Nations Office on Drugs and Crime. Used by permission.

Printed in the United States of America

7 6 5 4 3 2 1

To Jacob and Elyse Singer, mijos.

Contents

Preface

This book is the fourth in a series of volumes I have written, and Waveland Press has published, on the use, health and social impact, and underlying social causes of mood and mind-altering psychotropic drugs. The perspective taken in all of these books is that of critical medical anthropology (CMA). These books, each written to address a different aspect of human involvement with mood and mind-altering chemicals, seek to contribute to the understanding of why people use drugs, the social contexts and changing patterns of use over time (and in different places), the health and social consequences of drug use, the nature of the global drug trade, and the development and enforcement of drug policies, in terms of the complex social environments and structures of social relationships in which these behaviors are embedded, especially the significant role played by social inequality and the enactment of power in human affairs. Central to my approach is a deep appreciation, on the one hand, of the traditional anthropological focus on understanding the intricacies of local experiences, conditions, relationships, and practices and, on the other, the discipline's more recent concern with the connection of these to "processes [like colonialism, class structure, labor markets, globalism, advertising, the mass media] that transcend separate cases" (Wolf 1982:114).

In the first book in this series, called *Something Dangerous: Emergent and Changing Illicit Drug Use and Community Health* (2006), the focus is on *drug use dynamics*, a term I use to refer to the continual processes of change in drug use patterns.

The second book in the series, *The Face of Social Suffering: Life History of a Street Drug Addict* (2006), moves from the examination of systemic social processes to a narrowed and sharpened focus on drug use behavior, including its causes and consequences, by way of an examination of the troubled life of a street drug user in Hartford, CT.

The third book, *Drugging the Poor: Legal and Illegal Drugs and Social Inequality* (2007), extends the critical medical understanding of drug use beyond illicit drugs to the fuller pattern of intertwined legal and illegal drug use, with a special focus on the social groups that are involved in production and distribution, the economic system in which these entities operate, and the contributions of drug use to maintaining social inequality.

Drugs and Development broadens the critical analysis developed in the previous books by examining the impact of legal and illegal drug distribution and use on relations among richer and poorer nations, in particular their influence on social and economic development in the Third World. In a globalized world, one in which people, ideas, organizations, and commodities (including drugs), flow rapidly from place to place, and in which all places are tied together through the market, through advanced communication systems, and through rapid transportation technologies, drug distribution and use both reflect and reinforce an exploitive political economy that has connected the West and the other countries and regions (especially the so-called developing nations) of the world since the rise of capitalism. Drugs, in short, play an important, if complex, role in what the anthropologically influenced economist, historian, and world systems theorist Andre Gunder Frank called the "development of underdevelopment."

ACKNOWLEDGEMENTS

This book grew out of a speaking tour on global drug patterns in 2006, sponsored by the School of Anthropology, Geography and Environmental Studies, University of Melbourne. The author thanks the UN Office of Drugs and Crime for the photographs used in the book; Nick Crofts, Director of Turning Point Alcohol and Drug Centre in Melbourne, for providing materials that were useful in first stimulating the development of this book; Richard Needle of the Global AIDS Program for inviting participation in drugs and HIV/AIDS prevention initiatives in Brazil and Vietnam; Tim Rhodes and the *International Journal of Drug Policy*; Hans Baer for facilitating travel to Australia and for over 30 years of productive collaboration in the development of critical anthropology; J. Bryan Page for his continued collaboration in writing on drug issues; Tom Curtin and Jeni Ogilvie, my editors and friends at Waveland Press; and Pamela Erickson for her enduring support and for carefully reading and commenting on earlier drafts of this and my other Waveland books.

Chapter One

The Impact of Drugs in the Developing World

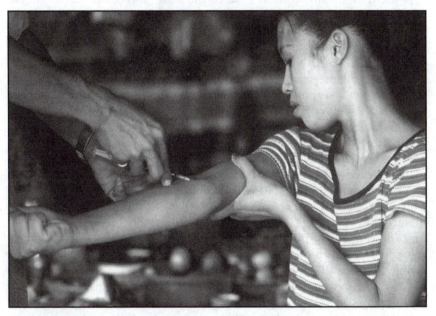

Young woman shooting up drugs in the slum area of Hanoi, Vietnam.
(Photo by Thomas Haily)

DEVELOPMENT IN AN IMPERFECT WORLD

In recent years, it has been said that development—the difficult to fully define process involving the growth and improvement of a nation or region technologically, economically, and socially—is about human rights, namely expanding freedoms, meeting pressing human

1

needs, and improving the quality of life. In advocating for a rights-based approach to development, the Asian Human Rights Commission and the People's Vigilance Committee for Human Rights (2006:1), for example, assert that "the true measure of development is not economic growth: it is human dignity." The emergence of this perspective, including its popular unification with participatory and ecological sustainability models, and its contestation with older, top-down economic approaches to development, point to the heart of the issues of concern discussed in this book, namely that "most people in the third world are [still] desperately poor. For them, the [twentieth century] promises of social change in the third world have not been kept" (Isbister 2006:1).

While various theories of the failures of development have been espoused, it is only recently that the role played by psychotropic drugs—including alcohol, tobacco, various pharmaceuticals, heroin, cocaine, methamphetamine and other mood and mind-altering substances—has been clear. Most importantly, what is beginning to be understood is that the ways such drugs—both as commodities and as political symbols—have been used and incorporated into relations among regions and nations over time constitute an important chapter in the story of development's failures.

While its roots can be traced to the seventeenth century (Wallerstein 1994), as a force in the contemporary world, development emerged in the aftermath of the Second World War, a Euro-centered global conflict that both inflicted enormous suffering and simultaneously unsettled international structures of colonial social control over what has come to be called the peoples of the Third World. Consequently, the starting point for understanding modern development—and the role drugs play for better or worse in this process—is in the colonial era and in the social and moral worlds created by colonialism around the planet.

While it is possible to use a label like "colonialism" to refer to a pattern of economic and political relationship between dominant and subordinate regions of the world—relations involving "the establishment of [p]olitical suzerainty over vast non-European areas . . . in order to safeguard the continued national interests of the European colonial nations" (Howell 2003:199)—without doubt colonialism had many faces. A glimpse of the colonial legacy for contemporary Third World development, and the resulting challenges that it created for expanding the quotient of dignity for ordinary people (including the ways drugs have figured into this heritage), can be seen through a telling example, that of Kaieteur Falls National Park and the country of Guyana.

The Troubling Case of Guyana

Deep in the tropical rainforest that blankets most of the Idaho-sized South American country of Guyana is found one of the most imposing and visually spectacular waterfalls in the world. With a free fall descent of over 700 feet, Kaieteur Falls has five times the elevation of the much better known Niagara Falls. The site was named for Kai, who was a chieftain of the indigenous Patamona people who have long dwelled in the region. Notably, in the Patamona language, *teur* means waterfall, while the name Guyana is derived from an Amerindian language term for "land of many waters." Naturalist Steve Fratello (2001) has depicted the area of the falls as an earthly paradise:

> Standing deep in the gorge on a white sand beach, with the dark waters of the Potaro roiling by, I've surveyed lush green glades of grasses and sedges that line rocky side channels of the river. I've watched as the Inga trees at the river's edge, their contorted branches heavily laden with epiphytes, attracted myriad butterflies and skippers to their delicate blossoms. Looking across the river to the billowing crowns of the mighty mora trees, I've let my gaze wander up the green slope to a smaller falls called Old Man's Beard, which cascades in tiers off the escarpment. All this plus Kaieteur Falls—if this isn't a paradise on earth, what is?

First described to the outside world in 1870 by European explorer, C. Barrington Browne, the falls and the surrounding country during the colonial era came under the purview of the British Colonial Administration, which designated the Potaro River area, including Kaieteur Falls, a national park in 1929.

While unique in its own ways, Guyana is something of an archetype of colonial history. First sighted by Columbus during his third voyage to the New World in 1498, it began to be settled by the Dutch in 1616. The British took over control late in the eighteenth century. During 150 years of colonial rule, which did not end until 1966, Britain, which was primarily focused on insuring the profitable operation of British-owned plantations and other businesses, reshaped Guyana's social reality. This complex restructuring involved multiple components, including importing first African slaves and later (following the abolition of slavery in 1834) East Indian laborers, setting off enduring interethnic conflict between Afro-Guyanese and Indo-Guyanese people by manipulating the living conditions of the local population (e.g., building or neglecting roads, bridges, and sanitation and irrigation facilities) to suit the economic interests of British planters; introducing English as the national language; bringing Western governance, religions, and moral structures to the country; and, through these sweeping changes, planting the broken seeds that would sprout a bitter developmental harvest for Guyana after independence (Seecoomar 2002).

Since the departure of the British, and the formation of the Cooperative Republic of Guyana, the park has been supervised by the Kaieteur Board and National Parks Commission of Guyana. Like many other government programs in Guyana, the commission is inadequately funded, understaffed by ill-trained workers, hobbled by the absence of a comprehensive management plan, and threatened by outside interests, especially the mining industry. Further, lack of adequate park staffing and the clandestinity offered by the thick forest vegetation make the park an appealing place for illicit marijuana cultivation and the transport of drugs by illicit traffickers.

The park suffers because Guyana is an underdeveloped nation in every sense of the word. As a result, with regard to the issue of human dignity, Guyana is anything but paradise. With a per capita gross domestic product of under $1,000, it is in fact one of the poorest countries in the Western Hemisphere. In 2006, the average income was $4,700 a year, with an unemployment rate thought to be over 10 percent. The overall infant mortality rate hovers at about 32 per 1,000 live births (although for low-income families it is over 70 per 1,000), and life expectancy is 66 years—compared to 22 deaths per 1,000 live births and a life expectancy of 75 years in neighboring Venezuela. By comparison, for a developed country like the United States—which actually has comparatively poor life statistics for a "modern" nation— the infant mortality rate is 6 per 1,000 live births and life expectancy is 78 years (CIA 2007). HIV/AIDS is a major problem in Guyana, with AIDS-related deaths among 15–34-year-olds pushing the country's death rate up by two and one-half times what it would be without the epidemic. Although not the primary cause of the spread of the epidemic in some Third World countries, directly and indirectly drugs play a significant role in the spread of HIV/AIDS in Guyana.

The cause of underdevelopment in Guyana is not a lack of resources to support social and economic advancement. Indeed, the nation is rich in timber, gold, diamonds, rice, sugar, fish, and bauxite, a mineral used in the production of aluminum. Rather, the historic fractures of colonialism and continued burdens of a weak national governing structure in what is a peripheral region of the world economy are critical factors in Guyanese underdevelopment. Part and parcel of this heritage is the place of Guyana in the netherworld of international drug trafficking. In a 2006 annual review, the U.S. State Department reported that the illicit drug trade comprises as much as 60 percent of all economic activity in Guyana and a "norm of illegality" exists in the country. University of Guyana political scientist Freddie Kisson labels the country "a mini narco-state," a designation for countries in which illegal drugs account for over half the gross national product (Wilkinson 2006).

Notably, the murder rate in Guyana is three times higher than that of the United States (U.S. Department of State 2007) and much of the violence is attributed to drug-related gangs. On April 22, 2006, for example, Guyana's agriculture minister, two of his two siblings, and a body guard were shot and killed in an apparent drug-related robbery. Stemming from the drug trade, and its common characteristics as an underground industry, in March of 2006 gunmen killed five printers at the *Kaieteur News*, the most popular daily newspaper in the country. The workers were forced to lie face down on the cement floor and were then shot in the back of the head. The gangland-style slaying, which was presumed to be retaliation by illicit drug corporations for undesirable news coverage of the drug trade, shocked the nation. In a statement to a special session of the twenty-fourth UN General Assembly, Navin Chandarpal (2000), a special envoy of the president of Guyana, emphasized that a major threat to the country's development

> is the steady increase in violence, crime and the trafficking and abuse of illicit drugs. The drug trade does not only corrupt individuals and systems by the enormity of its inducement but also threatens governance within our very country. Offenders, although largely youths, comprise all age groups with grandmothers being used in some cases, as "mules" for the drug trade. Once again, this phenomenon has been attributed to unfulfilled desires for a better way of life, propelled clearly by the insouciant images of wealth portrayed by the television and mass media.

While drug use and the drug trade have major impacts on the development of countries with a strong resource base like Guyana, for resource-poor countries, like several cases described in this book, they can be particularly damaging, indeed overwhelming to that point that the capacity for development is severely harmed.

Overview of the Book

Understanding the ways and degree to which drugs impact Third World development, both in terms of general, transnational patterns but also with regard to the specific and varied nature of the consequences for individual nations in the underdeveloped world, is the focus of this book. Research, for example, suggests that the drug trade played a significant role in recent economic crises in various Third World countries, including Mexico (1994–1995), Thailand (1997), Nigeria (2000–2002), and Argentina (2000–2002). As noted by the United Nations Educational, Scientific and Cultural Organization (Schiray and Fabre 2002):

> The social transformations stemming from the development of the drug economy reveal a growth in the sectors of illegal activity and their interpenetration with the official sectors of society. They involve the law and the norms and elementary rules of economic and social organization, and they seem to be causing a far-reaching shift in the pattern of development of our societies.

The effects of legal and illegal drug use and trafficking on development are not fully known, in part because these issues have not been thoroughly assessed. Addressing the growing involvement of illicit groups living in several West African nations in the transshipment of drugs from Asia and Latin America to Europe, for example, the United Nations Information Service (2002) reports "drug trafficking, related organized crime, and its destabilizing impact on the . . . democratization, stability and development process in Africa are still neglected phenomena."

While this book focuses on providing an account of the role of legal and illegal drugs on national social and economic development around the world, as the Guyana case suggests, in and of themselves drugs, while an important barrier to development in many places, are *by no means the full story of Third World underdevelopment*. Rather, to truly grasp the distressing contribution of drugs to underdevelopment it is necessary to introduce a broader political economic outlook that examines interactions between global drug distribution and use and other structural and historic factors in play on the world stage, while addressing critical questions like: (1) Why do flows of illicit drugs emerge and who benefits from their development? (2) Why is it difficult for Third World countries to resist enmeshment in the illicit drug trade? (3) What is the appeal of drugs and the drug trade in underdeveloped countries? (4) What effect do legal drugs have on national development?

To adequately answer these questions requires an understanding of "the development of underdevelopment" (Frank 1966), the colonial legacy in countries like Guyana, and the impact of contemporary globalization (e.g., the development of a market-based, corporate-driven world economy, the global electronic communication system, and the international transportation system) as facilitators of the legal and illegal drug industries. In other words, to move beyond the glib pronouncements of pundits and politicians about narco-states, narco-terrorists, and narco-development to fully realize the complex effects of drug use, addiction, and trade on development, it is necessary to take a comprehensive approach that views these phenomena in historic, social, and political economic contexts.

THE ROLE OF DRUGS IN THE DEVELOPMENT OF UNDERDEVELOPMENT

Conflicted Motives

The birth of the development movement as a global initiative among underdeveloped nations can be traced to the 1955 conference of Asian and African nations at Bandung, Indonesia, that led to the establishment of the Non-Aligned Movement bloc. As conceived there and afterwards, development is a tripartite project of modernization involving national changes in the economy, social organization, and governance. Since its inception, the international development program has been both driven and hindered by the fact that we live at a time in which large sectors of the world's population suffer from the intertwined plagues of poverty, inequality, and health disparities. The historic determinants of these scourges are of critical importance to understanding why they have endured as well as the role of drugs in their persistence.

For the developed nations, development of the Third World—from Latin America, to Africa, to Asia, to the Pacific—has had very clear if different motivations than those found in the underdeveloped world. As Frank (1991) has observed, "If anthropology was the child of imperialism and colonialism . . . [see Rylko-Bauer et al. 2006], then [in the West] development thinking was the child of neo-imperialism and neo-colonialism." It emerged during a time of urgency after the Second World War when the "new postwar American hegemony" (Frank 1991) began to seem at risk. The older European colonial powers had exhausted themselves in the war, while the United States had come out of the conflict largely unscathed and in possession of unprecedented levels of economic and military might. Moreover, unlike earlier periods in its history, the U.S. emerged from the war with global designs. The world—and all of its resources, markets, and laboring masses, now situated in new and emergent nations rather than historically divided colonial territories—appeared ripe for neoimperial picking by the world's new powerhouse. Henry Luce, publisher of *Time* magazine, described the period as the beginning of the "American Century," a time during which the United States could shape events to meet its global aspirations.

This bubble of optimism, however, was burst by the Chinese revolution of 1949, a social tidal wave that swept up a quarter of the world's population, sending a shock wave across the American business class. Other anticapitalist revolutionary struggles, such as occurred in Cuba, intensified this nervousness about the prospects for unfettered global revenue. As Frank (1991) aptly comments, "Developing a more harmless alternative became a matter of the greatest urgency, especially in the newly hegemonic United States." Thus was born Western support of Third World development. Its primary goal was not the elimination of the intertwined plagues of poverty, inequality, and health disparities, but rather it was making the world safe for reaping profit. The reason for this orientation is simple: "Economic development in underdeveloped countries is profoundly inimical to the dominant interests in the advanced capitalist countries" (Baran 1962:11). Thus, in his inaugural address to the nation on January 20, 1949, President Harry Truman stated:

More than half the people of the world are living in conditions
approaching misery. Their food is inadequate. They are victims of
disease. Their economic life is primitive and stagnant. Their
poverty is a handicap and a threat both to them and to more
prosperous areas. (Avalon Project 1997)

Enter Neoliberalism

Concern for the grave risk to developed nations of the Third
World's embrace of socialism and consequent rejection of participation
in the emergent, Western-dominated global economy soon led to the
creation of a number of powerful institutions, including the International Monetary Fund (IMF), the World Bank, and the World Trade
Organization. Each of these had a specific order-maintaining mission
on the global scene: the IMF was assigned the task of averting economic crises, like the Depression of the 1930s; the World Bank was
designed to facilitate development by making loans to poor countries;
and the World Trade Organization was charged with reducing or eliminating tariffs or other policies that limited the free flow of goods (and
profits). Following the Debt Crisis of the late 1970s to mid-1980s, a
period during which many Third World countries that had received
large development loans from the World Bank and the International
Monetary Fund or directly from developed nations were unable to
make payments on their debts, IMF and World Bank economists concluded that the primary barrier to development (and, hence to loan
repayment) was that "the state played too great a role in the economy,
inhibiting markets and firms from operating in a manner that would
raise overall welfare" (Gershman and Irwin 2000:22).

Consequently, various "structural adjustment" demands, reflec-
tive of the neoliberal economic thinking guiding the global development initiative (i.e., the belief that the market not intervention
programs will solve social problems like poverty and inequality), were
placed on debtor nations. Structural Adjustment Policies (SAPs)
included demands for sweeping reductions in the role and activities of
the state that were said to: retard "market forces" from setting pre-
vailing prices, limit the free flow of commodities, block foreign investment, or provide services that could be sold on the open market. In the
underdeveloped island nation of Haiti, for example, note Farmer and
Bertrand, the World Bank and the IMF developed an economic development plan that

> bore the marks of a SAP—namely, the cutting of government
> bureaucracies and public programs, the privatization of publicly
> owned utilities and industries, the promotion of exports, and an
> "open-investment policy" that would slash tariffs and eliminate any
> import restrictions that might trammel investors, especially those
> of the foreign variety. (2000:82)

Although the Haiti government under the popular rule of President Jean-Bertrand Aristide resisted the shift toward structural adjustment, when, with U.S. support, Aristide was overthrown in 2004, most of the safety net and development programs developed by his government, such as subsidized rice for the poor, literacy centers, and water supply projects, came to a grinding halt. By the early 1990s, over 70 nations had accepted SAPs and received new adjustment loans, while services and safety net protections for the poor, and hence their standard of living, crumbled.

The Enduring Colonial Legacy

Despite these programs and adjustments, as the development effort picked up momentum, the magnitude of the challenges it faced became increasingly clear. One source of these challenges, as seen in the earlier discussion of Guyana, is what has been referred to as the "colonial legacy." Observes Frank (1966):

> It is also widely believed that the contemporary underdevelopment of a country can be understood as the product or reflection solely of its own economic, political, social, and cultural characteristics or structure. Yet historical research demonstrates that contemporary underdevelopment is in large part the historical product of past and continuing economic and other relations between the satellite underdeveloped and the now developed metropolitan countries. Furthermore, these relations are an essential part of the structure and development of the capitalist system on a world scale as a whole.

Colonialism was a fundamental component of the relations among underdeveloped and developed nations to which Frank refers. During the colonial era, as noted with reference to Guyana, existing economic patterns and political arrangements in dominated territories were restructured to serve the interests of the colonial powers; that is, they were reorganized to facilitate the extraction and export of wealth (which was used, notably, to pay for the further development of Western nations). Thus, "development" during this era, such as the building up of capital cities, the construction of roads or dams in the countryside, or the development of irrigation systems and the transformation of agriculture from food-crop to mono-cash crop production, was designed to serve foreign economic interests rather than contribute to internal social and economic improvement.

For example, with reference again to Haiti, which had been a New World French colony, Ary Bordes (1979:17) writes of the "oppressive legacy from our former masters, thirsty for profits, and little interest in the living conditions and health of the indigenous people." Similarly, with regard to colonial India, a former British dependency, Shishir Thadani (2007) comments on the sometimes asserted contributions of colonial nations:

It is undoubtedly true that the British built modern cities with modern conveniences for their administrative officers. But it should be noted that these were exclusive zones not intended for the "natives" to enjoy. Consider that in 1911, 69 per cent of Bombay's population lived in one-room tenements (as against 6 per cent in London in the same year). The 1931 census revealed that the figure had increased to 74 per cent—with one-third living more than 5 to a room.

In many parts of the world, an enduring aspect of the colonial legacy was the division of regions into manageable colonial states whose boundaries were established without consideration of where particular peoples lived, how they were organized socially and politically, and the nature of their indigenous identities, languages or cultures (Achebe 1984, Meredith 1984). Thus, reflecting on his home country and "the well-known arbitrariness of [postcolonial] frontiers" (Anderson 2006:114), Nigerian nationalist, Chief Obafemi Awolowo observes:

> Nigeria is not a nation. It is a mere geographical expression. There are no "Nigerians" in the same sense as there are "English," "Welsh," or "French." The word "Nigerian" is merely a distinctive appellation to distinguish those who live within the boundaries of Nigeria and those who do not. (Amadi 2007)

Similarly, as Anderson (2006:120) points out with reference to the far-flung nation of Indonesia, "as its hybrid pseudo-Hellenic name suggests, its stretch does not remotely correspond to any precolonial domain; on the contrary . . . its boundaries [for the most part were those] left behind by the last Dutch conquests."

Internal Conflict as a Legacy of Colonialism

Often, the lack of any sense of national unity has been the basis for intense conflict in postcolonial countries. As starkly expressed by Makwec Kuol Makwec, a Dinka tribal chief with allusion to differences between northern and southern people in war-torn Sudan, "we have never been one, we will never be one" (quoted in Jok 2007:2). Similarly, in Nigeria since the brutal civil war of 1967–1970, the country "has remained in a state of suppressed, 'silent' or 'repressed' violence punctuated by periodic outbursts of actual violence, some causing significant casualties and making thousands of refugees in their own country" (Ibeanu and Luckham 2007:42). Even emergent countries that were said to have the resources needed to succeed have fallen victim to internal strife. A British colony from 1796 until 1948, Sri Lanka (known as Ceylon until 1972), for example, was considered to be one of "the most promising candidates for stable statehood and development of the 'new states' emerging from decolonized Africa and Asia" (Bose 2007:12). By 1984, however, tension between Tamil and

Sinhalese ethnic groups had escalated into full-scale civil war. Indeed, in many colonial lands, internal clashes and animosities across ethnic lines were fostered by colonial regimes as part of a strategy of divide and conquer.

As a consequence of such practices, border wars with neighboring nations (often stemming from tensions inherent in the fact that ethnic groups were divided by imposed national boundaries) have continually sapped the energy of Third World countries. Moreover, colonial administrations did not foster internal political and social development (e.g., through promoting literacy and public education or advancing the development of a democratic civil society), nor did they invest in developing an economic, legal, educational, and political infrastructure that could support postcolonial development (Soyinka 1996). On the contrary, often colonial administration insured postcolonial struggles and internal strife, with painful cost to the people of emergent underdeveloped nations. Writing several years ago of Nigeria, for example, Windstone (2002:1) noted:

> While the ruling military class devises ever more incredible and ingenious ways to bankrupt the nation and extract funds from any international agencies or corporations willing to gamble on its future, living conditions of the Nigerian people grow ever more abysmal, [with] hundreds of thousands of youths roam[ing] the streets, jobless, without purpose or direction.

It is precisely these kind of youth to whom drugs appeal, and it is not surprising therefore that Nigeria has played a prominent role in drug trafficking between Asia and Europe. To these youth, drugs promise something better—a more exciting life, a chance to be admired, relief from distress, a pathway to modernity.

Eras of Globalization

Exacerbating the fragility of state institutions in politically independent but underdeveloped nations in the post–World War II period have been the transformative forces of globalization, the very process so effectively promoted by the International Monetary Fund, the World Bank, and the World Trade Organization. Economists are in general agreement that there have been two waves of modern globalization, the first began in the mid-nineteenth century or even earlier and continued until the mid-twentieth century, and the second began in the mid-twentieth century and continues today. As Patten (2001) observes:

> More than 100 years ago, in *The Ballad of East and West*, the British poet Kipling wrote a line of verse which would subsequently enter the English language almost as a cliché: "Oh, East is East, and West is West, and never the twain shall meet." Much has changed since then. . . . But the biggest change of all, the change

> that has and is touching more lives than even the world wars did,
> is the phenomenon known as globalisation. Of course, there is
> nothing new about globalisation. . . . The difference this time is its
> scope. . . . Not only is globalisation now reaching into a vastly great-
> er number of countries, it is also reaching into vastly greater areas
> of our lives.

The first wave of globalization, comprising the colonial era, contributed
significantly to a monumental shift from a world of independent and
diverse peoples and places to the tying together of the far-flung corners
of the world into an overarching economic and, within the colonial
regimes, political system. The second wave of globalization, born in the
aftermath of the Second World War, has involved the "creation of new
economic, financial, political, cultural, and personal relationships
through which societies and nations come into closer and novel types of
contact with one another" (Waters 2001:80). More precisely, contemporary globalization involves

> transnational capitalist economic processes, including resource
> extraction and trade, which override local decision making, tradi-
> tional ways of life, and indigenous cultural histories and push
> toward uniformities, the imposition of externally devised social
> changes, and the elevation of the market and the needs of transna-
> tional corporations as the socially legitimized determinant of social
> value and ways of life. (Singer 2007:10)

The Collapse of Governance

One of the places globalization processes have reached and had
notable impact is in the authority of national governments of Third
World countries. There has been in many of these countries, as Kaldor
and coauthors (2007:3) stress, a "gradual disintegration of the state
under the impact of globalism." Exemplary is the government of Nigeria, which has largely been unable "to counter the powerful market
forces and economic incentives driving violence" in the country
(Ibeanu and Luckham 2007:42). Given its oil-based economy, and the
great wealth that oil makes available (even if most of it flows out of
Nigeria to the multinational oil companies like Mobil, Chevron, Shell,
Elf, and Agip), it might have seemed that Nigeria would be able to sustain a strong, well-funded central government. The opposite has been
the case. Observes Polgreen (2006:1), "The world's growing thirst for
African oil is creating a tangled and often bloody web of conflict
marked by poverty and a near abdication of responsibility by government in countries like Nigeria." In the characterization of British
political economist Susan Strange (1995:56): "state authority has
leaked away upwards, sideways and downward." Strange further
states, increasingly Third World states are

becoming hollow, or defective, institutions. To outward appearances unchanged, the inner core of their authority in society and over economic transactions within their defined territorial borders is seriously impaired. They are like old trees, hollow in the middle, showing signs of weakness and vulnerability to storm, drought, or disease, yet continuing to grow leaves, new shoots, and branches. Some are clearly more defective in terms of their ability to play their roles in society, further advanced in decrepitude, than others. But the structural forces bringing about the hollowing of state authority are common to all, and it is hard to envisage a reversal of the trends. (1995:56)

As a result of the dual and mutually reinforcing consequences produced by the colonial legacy and the processes of globalization, underdeveloped nations are highly vulnerable to the considerable economic power wielded by both legal and illegal drug corporations. The governmental structures of many Third World countries, in fact, are now so weak that they have been labeled "fragile" (or even "failed") states in the development discourse. Fragile states are defined as countries with governments that cannot or will not deliver core functions to their populations, except for the elite. They lack the will or the capacity to manage public resources, deliver basic services, and protect poor and vulnerable groups. At the most extreme level, such as transpired in Haiti in recent years, there is a "collapse of state institutions, especially the police and judiciary, with resulting paralysis of governance, a

Opium poppy cultivation in Afghanistan.

breakdown of law and order, and general banditry and chaos" (Thürer 1999:731). Currently, 46 countries have been listed as fragile or failing states by international development organizations (Ranson et al. 2007).

Often overlooked in discussions in developed countries, international lending institutions, donor organizations, and multinational corporations about the nature of fragile or failed states is the significant contribution of all of these dominant global actors in producing Third World state vulnerability. Consequently, the historic role of political economic relations between First and Third World countries in creating the conditions that facilitate the development of narco-states, international drug trafficking, and developmental toll produced by drugs is obscured.

DRUGS AS BARRIERS TO DEVELOPMENT

Since the middle of the twentieth century, development ideology and terminology have gone through various permutations. Societies long referred to in the West as "backward" or even uncivilized came to be called "undeveloped" and later, in light of the fact that this label was no less pejorative than its predecessor, "underdeveloped." Subsequently, this term also fell into disfavor and was replaced first by "less developed countries" and then by "developing countries." In short, the world came to be defined as being comprised of two types of nations, developed and developing, with the implication being that the latter were following in the footsteps of the former and would emerge (someday) as modern countries with market-centered economies and Western-style political systems.

Current international development orthodoxy, which has come to recognize the important hindrance to development of poverty, inequality, and health disparity, now focuses on achieving what have been termed the Millennium Development Goals (MDGs), an ambitious set of objectives adopted at the United Nations Summit of world leaders in the year 2000. At that historic meeting, 189 heads of state and their representatives entered into a global agreement to "free our fellow men, women, and children from the abject and dehumanising conditions of extreme poverty" by 2015. Specifically, the MDG pact officially committed the international community to: eradicating extreme poverty and hunger, achieving universal primary education, promoting gender equality and empowering women, achieving a significant reduction in infant and maternal mortality, gaining control of infectious diseases such as HIV/AIDS and malaria, protecting environmental quality, and developing a global partnership of rich and poor nations for sustainable development.

The issue of drug use and trafficking, a concern that generally is overlooked in the development debate (Andreas 2004), and not much addressed in the literature on the Millennium Development Goals, places serious constraints on the ability of underdeveloped nations to achieve sustainable improvement across the full range of accepted development goals. The relationship between psychotropic drugs and development is rooted in the contribution that the legal and illegal drug trade makes to a set of health and social barriers to development, including: (1) the lowering of worker productivity (and, thus, the resources to invest in development) as a result of the skewing of economies toward drug production (and money laundering) and away from a meaningful focus on development; (2) the ensnarement of youth into drug distribution and away from productive education or employment (thereby lowering the sustainability of development over time); (3) the emergence of new or enhanced health problems (that diminish participation in development efforts); (4) the corruption of public servants and the disintegration of social institutions (which undercut program operations and increases the spread of corruption to individual development programs); and (5) interpersonal crime and community violence (which disrupt development initiatives and diminish the trust and commitment needed to maintain development efforts). Each of these impacts of drug use and trafficking will be examined in more detail in chapter 3.

Only in recent years, in fact, has it come to be recognized that for development programs to be effective, policy makers require a far better understanding of the relationship between drugs and social and economic development. As noted by Jan Kavan of the Czech Republic in 2003, while serving as president of the United Nations General Assembly:

> Drug abuse is a global problem. . . . Drug trafficking knows no boundaries. An estimated 200 million people worldwide consume illicit drugs. Drug abuse furthers socio-economic and political instability, it undermines sustainable development, and it hampers efforts to reduce poverty and crime. (Kavan 2003:1)

Drugs—including those that are legal as well as those that are not, their consumption, their movement, and also the public promotion of legal drug use by corporate manufacturers—have, within the broader context of the colonial legacy and globalization, emerged as primary barriers to development in many countries. This, however, has not been fully or effectively analyzed as a development obstacle despite the considerable attention given to issues like technological development and economic growth in the contemporary world.

CHALLENGES OF THE MILLENNIUM
DEVELOPMENT GOALS

Achievement of the MDGs would significantly improve the lot of the poor and reduce social suffering and structural inequality in the world. Seemingly toward this end, there has been a steady rise in aid from developed to developing countries, reaching over $100 billion in 2005. Closer examination, however, reveals that more than half of this aid is debt relief on the billions of dollars already owed by poor countries to rich ones. Debt relief does not increase the amount of money that is spent on eradication of poverty or on the achievement of any of the other development goals. Additionally, a large part of the remaining aid money now goes into emergency and disaster relief, such as aid following the devastating Indian Ocean tsunami of 2004. While relief addresses the immediate needs of the victims of disaster, it does not tend to address long-term developmental objectives. Additionally, not all aid to underdeveloped nations is earmarked for development efforts; military aid, for example, contributes little to national development and may foster border conflicts that further deplete resources for development. Further, according to the UN Department of Economic and Social Affairs (2006), the 50 least-developed nations receive only about one-third of all aid that flows from developed countries. In other words, aid does not tend to move from rich to poor countries on the basis of development need, but rather from rich countries to their closest allies, whatever their development status.

As a result of these factors, all of which reflect socioeconomic and sociopolitical relations among nations, questions have been raised about the commitment of highly developed nations to the MDGs, or, more precisely: what might be the prioritized motivations behind support for the MDGs among developed nations (Amir 2006, Black and White 2004)? In the assessment of Bernard Founou-Tchuigoua (2002) the MDGs are less about real development than they are a reflection of a new phase in asymmetrical structural adjustment. Notes Founou-Tchuigoua (2002:25), the MDG agreement promises that

> the twenty-first century will be distinguished by a new cooperation from which unilateral interference from the colonial and postcolonial period will be banned: it is the key concept of Partnership. But instead of reducing the . . . [problems of] the structural adjustment era, the . . . [new partnerships] reinforce them and in reality suggest a framework which allows . . . [developed] states an interference which surpasses the economy and even the social to include the politics.

One measure of donor commitment is that sufficient funds are provided to allow for the accomplishment of targeted goals (Fukuda-Parr 2004). To describe the level of progress that has been made in achieving the MDG, in 2006 the United Nations released a Millennium Development Goals Report. The report summarizes the status of affairs with regard to each of the development goals. Regarding the eradication of extreme poverty and hunger, or as the goal is precisely stated, "between 1990 and 2015, [halving] the proportion of people who suffer from hunger," the report finds:

> Chronic hunger—measured by the proportion of people lacking the food needed to meet their daily needs—has declined in the developing world. But progress overall is not fast enough to reduce the number of people going hungry. . . . The worst-affected regions—sub-Saharan Africa and Southern Asia—have made progress in recent years. But their advances have not kept pace with those of the early 1990s, and the number of people going hungry is increasing. (UN Department of Economic and Social Affairs 2006:7)

Similarly, regarding the eradication of HIV, the report notes that while the rate of new HIV infections has slowed in some developing nations, "rates of infection overall are still growing . . . [a]nd the number of people living with HIV has continued to grow" (UN Department of Economic and Social Affairs 2006:16).

Beyond the limited progress that has been made in the achievement of the development goals during the first third of the proposed target period (i.e., 2000–2015), the UN report notes that with an annual rate in urban migration of about 4.6 percent, 2007 will mark the first time in human history that the majority of people on the earth live in urban areas. Not only are cities growing in developing nations, so are the slum areas of Third World cities. In the rapidly expanding urban slums of impoverished countries, rural-to-urban migrants face poverty, lack of housing, overcrowding, inadequate water and sanitation, and street violence. In particular, youth unemployment rates in developing nations, countries that contain over 80 percent of the youth in the world today, have continued to rise since the launch of the MDG. As the UN report (2006:25) affirms, "Without sufficient employment opportunities, many young people grow discouraged and feel worthless." This set of conditions, combined with increased access to both legal and illegal drugs in all Third World cities as a result of globalism and international support for the free flow of goods, has created a situation that appears ripe for significant increases in mood-altering drug use and their associated health problems. Given suggestions that the highest priority objectives of developed nations express self-interest rather than the identified needs of undeveloped countries, there is growing concern in sectors of the international public health community that existing funding and policy decisions may foster rather than retard drug use, which, in turn, may further undermine progress toward achieving development goals.

Guided by a critical political economic perspective that locates local development efforts within the context of the colonial legacy, contemporary globalization, and the operation of global drug economies, and focusing on developing nations in Asia, Africa, the Pacific, the Caribbean and Latin America, the remaining chapters of this book examine: (1) the nature of mind-altering drug consumption, the levels and kinds of drug use and abuse across nation-states and regions, and the appeal of drugs in the developing world; (2) health and social problems associated with the use of legal and illegal drugs; (3) the ways in which drug use impacts and impairs development, including the corrupting influences of drug trafficking and legal drug company adoption of illegal marketing strategies; and (4) the failure of existing control strategies and the need for new approaches for diminishing the burden placed by drugs and drug trafficking on development.

Chapter Two

Global Drug Capitalism

Drug shipment seized by the Drug Control Agency of Tajikistan.

This chapter explores the emergence of legal and illegal drugs as commodities in light of the worldwide impact of the first and second waves of globalization, or what Swedish anthropologist, Signe Howell (2003), with the intent of calling attention to both continuities and discontinuities in global relations of inequality, refers to, respectively, as "old-style colonialism" and "new-style globalization." Continuities in the transition from colonialism to globalization stem from the fact that both involve engagement of the local with far wider social and economic systems (although these become ever more complex forms of interaction over time); discontinuities, such as the erasure of the relevance of distance, as communication and transport technologies advance, produce changes that are much more than "old wine in new wine skins."

THE EMERGENCE OF DRUGS
AS GLOBAL COMMODITIES

Historically, it is clear that drugs have played a far greater role in the structuring national and international social relations and hence in the creation of the modern world than is often recognized (Jankowiak and Bradburd 2003). This process began during the first wave of globalism. During this era, world powers like England (in Europe, India, and China) and France (in Southeast Asia) made significant contributions to the international spread of drug production and use. This, in turn, helped to pay for the further technological and social development of Europe. Drugs like heroin and cocaine, which previously were produced through local manufacture primarily for local consumption in indigenous communities and micropopulations around the world, were transformed into psychotropic drugs produced explicitly as commodities for sale within an important sector of the global economy that I have called drug capitalism (Singer 2007).

Until the late nineteenth century and culminating in the early twentieth century, drug capitalism, in all its expressions, was a fully legal enterprise, at which point national laws and international agreements (as discussed in chapter 4) led to some drugs being banned (e.g., heroin and cocaine), while others that are no less risky or addictive (e.g., tobacco, alcohol, pharmaceutical psychotropics) remained and continue to remain legal commodities. At the point of fracture into lawful and unlawful drugs, national and (increasingly) transnational corporations emerged as the primary players in the production and distribution of legal drug commodities (although some governments are involved as well), while various outlaw groups gained control of the international production and distribution of illegal drug commodities. The latter groups include the mafioso and Cosa Nostra in Sicily and the U.S., the mafiyas in the former Soviet Union, the cocaine cartels in Colombia, the Triads in China, and the Yakusa in Japan. In practice, and increasingly in terms of organization, however, legal and illicit drug corporations appear to have many more parallels than differences, except for several characteristics that stem directly from their legal status, and hence I have argued for the use of the term "drug corporation" to cover both entities (Singer 2007). Drug capitalism, in sum, is a complex multitrillion dollar global enterprise populated by various sanctioned and prohibited profit-making organizations dedicated to the manufacture, movement, and marketing of drug commodities.

Coca (cocaine)
cultivation in
Colombia.

Drugs transition from being local consumable goods into consumable commodities when they are exchanged (e.g., sold, traded, etc.). As the anthropologist, Arjun Appadurai (1986:3) argues, "Economic exchange creates value. Value is embodied in commodities that are exchanged." Drugs, which are readily tradable, constitute *consumable psychotropic commodities*, that is, chemical substances that are industrially produced through a system of wage labor and commercially distributed in a market economy. Notably, in the drug trade, drug commodities acquire greater value the farther they move from the actual hands that first produced them. The drug chain begins with the farmers who plant and tend the plants, which are then transported to the workers in hidden drug laboratories who chemically process them into a concentrated consumable or near consumable state. From the labs, they reach higher-level national or regional drug dealers who arrange their movement and distribution in bulk to drug smugglers. The smugglers transport the drugs from country of origin to country of sale, to various middle-level dealers who move drugs into particular communities. Within these communities are street-level vendors who sell small allotments of drugs to often fervent consumers. All along the way in this chain of distribution, further changes may be made to drug commodities, often of the sort that increases their street value by decreasing purity (a process that involves mixing other, usually nonpsychotropic, substances of far lesser value in with the drugs). As a result of these factors, cocaine, for example, increases in value as much as 15,000 percent as it travels from the hands of small farmers to those of street drug consumers.

Commodities do not come into existence automatically; rather, they are borne of social processes that are expressions of various kinds of social relationship (e.g., the unequal and potentially oppressive relations between the bosses and workers in an illicit drug lab) (Lyt-tleton 2006). In other words, drugs are "intentional," market-driven items of value that connect poor producers of raw substances to, often, poor consumers in distant lands across broad and complex global net-works, under the supervision of the captains (and real profit makers) of the drug industry.

While the nature of globalization is frequently framed by econo-mists as a product of unguided economic processes, for example as a result of supply and demand, as Navarro argues, global corporations "rely heavily on the government of the country in which they are based for creating the national and international conditions favorable to their reproduction and expansion" (2001:90). In other words, rather than narrow economic determinism, the shape and direction of globalism and commodity distribution are influenced by several political factors, including the policies enacted and actions taken by governments. In no small measure, the nature of these policies and the capacity of govern-ments to enforce them are shaped by the political economy of nations, that is, the historic location of a nation on the continuum between the dominant core and weaker periphery of the global economy (Baer, Singer, and Susser 2003; Wallerstein 1979). Weaker nations, including those encumbered by their colonial and postcolonial history of relations with dominant countries, are highly susceptible to penetration by the international drug trade, but essentially all nations, from the core to the periphery, participate in different ways in global drug flows.

DRUGS AND THE FIRST WAVE OF GLOBALISM

Historically, Europe, the center of the rise of globalization, was not a continent rich in the availability and use of psychotropic drugs other than alcohol. This changed during the first wave of globalization as European explorer/conquerors fanned out to the four corners of the world, motivated by the desire for fame, fortune, adventure, and the opportunity to spread the national faith and flag across the non-Euro-pean continents and peoples of color that inhabited them. A starting place for this transition was the introduction of tobacco to Europe from the New World during the sixteenth century. Opium, as well, played an important role in this process.

England, Tobacco, and Opium

The international tobacco industry began during the colonial era after Columbus returned from his voyage to the New World carrying a supply of leaves of the tobacco plants he "discovered" among indige-nous peoples of the Caribbean islands. During his transoceanic visits to the Caribbean, Columbus and his crews observed Arawakan-speaking local inhabitants smoking large, funnel-shaped cigars made up of a leaf that was completely unknown to the European adventurers. Having read the travel journals of Marco Polo, Columbus had hoped to find Cipangu (Japan) and fill his ships with items valued in Europe like gold and spices. He first recorded his awareness of tobacco in his journal on October 15, 1492, as his ships passed a small island that tellingly would be named Rum Cay:

> Being at sea, about midway between Santa Maria and the large island, which I name Fernandina, we met a man in a canoe going from Santa Maria to Fernandina; he had with him a piece of the bread which the natives make . . . and some dried leaves which are in high value among them, for a quantity of it was brought to me at San Salvador. (quoted in Mar 1996)

The Indians on the island of Hispaniola (known indigenously as Bohío but today is divided between the countries of Haiti and the Dominican Republic) explained to Columbus that they used the leaf, which they called "tabaco," to comfort their limbs after hard labor, to bring on sleep, and to lessen general body fatigue. Desperate to bring back something of value from his voyages to his benefactors Queen Isabella and King Ferdinand of Spain, Columbus introduced tobacco to Europe as a medicinal drug, and it was at first cultivated there for this purpose. Tobacco pipe smoking caught on among the upper class of England through the efforts of Sir Walter Raleigh, a smoker and influential figure in the royal court during the mid-sixteenth century.

By 1600, smoking had diffused to the working class, where it became a common practice in the port cities of England and Ireland. The appeal, very likely, was the same then as it is now among subordinated populations—a means of coping with the stresses and demands of being at the bottom of an oppressive class structure. As a comfort to working people, something that brought them together outside of the presence of the watchful eyes of the dominant social class, the practice came to be seen as a threat, especially among those concerned with controlling the behavior of the emergent and potential rebellious laboring class.

Although there was considerable resistance, including the passage of legal bans and restrictions on tobacco by many European countries, as well as stringent punishments for it use, by the end of the seventeenth century tobacco was legal and widely used throughout Europe. Britain, in particular, pushed for legalization throughout the continent because the soil of its Virginia colony proved to be an especially good medium for tobacco growth. Dried tobacco was lightweight and could be shipped across the ocean at comparatively low cost. The high demand for tobacco in England and the rest of Europe where it had become the modern and upwardly mobile thing to do—was sustained because of the addictive nature of nicotine. Addiction meant that the new commodity would attract a highly profitable sales volume. In due course, as recognition grew of the sizable revenue to be made by the state through taxing tobacco, greed overcame the initial fear of loss of control of a tobacco-emboldened working class and the laws and penalties for tobacco consumption largely passed into oblivion.

As a result, tobacco became an important force in national development in Europe through its role as a source of funds used to support the creation of a Western-centered global economy. Additionally, as Mintz (1985) points out, tobacco, like other colonial psychotropic substances, such as coffee and tea, was one of the "drug foods" that served as low-cost food substitutes for the laboring class of Europe during the rise of colonialism and the subsequent rise of the capitalist mode of production. By increasing "the worker's energy output and productivity, such substitutes figured importantly in balancing the accounts of capitalism" (Mintz 1985:148).

Through tobacco, the ruling class of Britain learned an important lesson, namely that trade in psychotropic commodities can be the source of great wealth. It was a lesson many others would learn in time as well. Learning this lesson began in 1773 when the British East India Company, a colonial trading firm, gained a monopoly over opium sales in all of India. By 1797, it had control over production as well. As colonial rulers, the British restructured Indian agricultural production to focus on two main cash crops: cotton and opium. The British colonial empire turned to opium production as a way of overcoming its balance of trade deficit with China. The British wanted various items produced by China, especially tea, but they had trouble finding something China wanted to buy from them in return. On the whole, the Chinese did not look favorably on Europeans or their goods. Consequently, from 1839 to 1842 Britain went to war with China to gain the right to export its Indian opium for use as a smokable drug by the Chinese people. The Chinese government resisted this attempt at overt drug imperialism but was defeated in what has since been called The First Opium War (1839–1842). Fifteen years later, Britain renewed its war against China in the Second Opium War, in order to extend its distribution of opium. In this way, the Chinese were "literally 'force fed' opium, and the supply continued to create its own demand" (Conrad and Schneider 1980:113). Yunnan Province became a center of opium production, with some of the product reaching international markets including the U.S. (Benedict 1996). This process was promoted by improvements in shipping technology but led, in turn, to the diffusion of "bubonic plague from the Yunnan reservoir into Vietnam and then into the global pathway" (Griffiths 2006:59), including San Francisco. By the end of the nineteenth century, it is estimated that one out of every ten Chinese was addicted to opium (Kittrie 1971). Meanwhile, Britain made significant profits, sufficient to attract the concern of the U.S., with which it was beginning to contend for world economic preeminence.

French Opium in Southeast Asia

A second country to learn the lesson of drug promotion was France, and its focus was on opium. Opium farming had been introduced to Southeast Asia by minority ethnic groups like the Yao that moved into the region fleeing the Opium Wars in China. After the French attacked southern Vietnam in 1858 and took over control of Saigon, the French quickly moved to establish colonial monopolies over opium production in the region (McCoy 1991). From a locally grown medicinal crop, opium was converted into a cash crop that "was responsible for a major part of French colonial revenues" (Boonwaat 2006:52). The French continued to push for increased production; as the quantity of opium produced went up, so did the number of people who became addicted to the drug. The drug was marketed to the public through government opium shops. Additionally, the French imported opium from India and taxed the sale of it to local customers. Based on the success of this venture, the French established a protectorate in Cambodia in 1883, annexed the Tonkin region of in central Vietnam in 1884, and claimed Laos in 1893, initially creating five separate French colonies in Indochina. The colonial administration of this complex system of control was costly and was largely paid for through the sale of opium. By 1918, there were over 3,000 opium retail outlets, over 1,500 opium dens, and an estimated 100,000 opium addicts in the region of French control (McCoy 1991, Reid and Costigan 2002).

This system was largely organized by Paul Doumer, a budget analyst who was appointed the governor-general of the French empire in Indochina. After consolidating opium purchasing, Doumer authorized the construction of a modern opium refinery in Saigon, which transformed raw opium from India into a high-grade smokable form. Like latter-day tobacco chemists, staff at the refinery concocted an opium blend that burned faster than regular opium, increasing user demand and opium profits. At the same time, employing modern niche marketing approaches, Doumer began buying cheaper Chinese opium and sold the lower-grade product to Vietnamese who could not afford the more expensive Indian opium brand.

During Doumer's four-year term, opium revenues increased by 50 percent and accounted for approximately one-third of colonial income. Funds from opium sales were invested in the development of infrastructure in the colony, including railroads, schools, and hospitals (Thompson 1968). So committed were the colonial rulers in Indochina to the opium trade that when international opposition to opium began to build during the 1920s and 1930s—led by the U.S. when felt it was being hurt economically by the British and French opium profits—the French vehemently resisted efforts to curb the Asian drug market (Naval Intelligence 1943).

After the Second World War, as the anticolonial communist movement led by Ho Chi Minh began to build, the colonial opium trade became a significant symbol of oppression. Ho Chi Minh (1961) reserved some of his sharpest criticism for French authorities involved in the opium industry, and the role of opium, as well as alcohol, in controlling the Vietnamese was mentioned in the Declaration of Independence from French colonial rule penned by Ho Chi Minh (1967). In a letter he wrote in 1920, Ho Chi Minh (1920) complained:

> You all have known that French imperialism entered Indochina half a century ago. In its selfish interests, it conquered our country with bayonets. Since then we have not only been oppressed and exploited shamelessly, but also tortured and poisoned pitilessly. Plainly speaking, we have been poisoned with opium, alcohol, etc.

To insure widespread distribution of their psychotropic product, the French built alcohol and opium houses in many villages (Duiker 2000). With large numbers of mine and plantation workers addicted to opium, and using much of their income to buy the drugs, the health effects were palpable. Workers were underfed and their gaunt bodies were emblematic of the consequences of external domination. Especially hard hit by opium addiction were the better educated Vietnamese whose capacities were sapped by the drug. A related consequence was corruption among government workers in need of cash to support their addiction (Dumarest 1938). In the end, the French were driven out of Vietnam, but were replaced by the U.S., which developed its own involvement in the opium trade.

In sum, during the first wave of globalism drugs played a significant role in development, fueling growth and expansion in Europe while already beginning the process of hindering similar developments in colonized countries. Although some profits from drug capitalism were used for development in European colonies, these expenditures were primarily driven by the needs of enhancing colonial administration and facilitating further extraction of profits from colonial holdings.

DRUGS AND THE SECOND WAVE OF GLOBALISM

As noted in chapter 1, one goal of the neoliberal policies promoted by Western nations and the development banks that have been so prominent during the second wave of globalism is the removal of all barriers to free trade to allow the unfettered flow of commodities across national boundaries. Among other effects these transformations, "dis-mantle[d] . . . economic controls inadvertently weaken[ing] the safe-guards, however ineffective, which . . . served to stem the expansion of drug trafficking activities in the past" (United Nations Office on Drugs and Crime 1994:13). As a consequence, the flow of both legal and illegal drugs has increased dramatically in many areas, despite the promotion of drug control efforts. For example, both Peru and Bolivia, major cocaine-producing countries, have adopted economic restructuring pro-grams that minimize government barriers and facilitate the flow of commodities. The War on Drugs, however, as discussed in chapter 4, puts pressure on countries to enhance their control programs (e.g., more rigorous border patrols, expanded military and court systems, enforcement of more stringent penalties for drug offenders) for combat-ing the flow of drugs. As Andreas (1995:75) points out, in Peru and Bolivia "compliance with neoliberal policy objectives has necessarily meant undermining U.S. drug policy objectives." Conversely, compli-ance with the War on Drugs, which in the case of Peru and Bolivia involves an emphasis on coca crop eradication programs, has resulted in a "progressive stripping away of the façade of the participatory and consensual nature of alternative development" and contributed to pop-ular resistance to alternative development schemes (Cohen 2006:34).

In recent years, in the context of neoliberal policies, it is notable that there has been a global dissemination of amphetamine-type stim-ulants (ATS), such as ecstasy. Lyttleton, in his analysis of Laos, for example, found that "socio-economic modernization and increased engagement in a globalized economy [have] create[d] new markets for synthetic drugs" like ATS. Popular interest in ATS "has emerged in sync with changing values systems fostered by specific development trajectories" (2006:22). Seen as a drug of developed nations, ATS use has become in Laos a cultural symbol of increased production, cash income, and a consumer culture oriented toward the pursuit of plea-sure through commodity acquisition; in a word its use has emerged as an expression of modernism. ATS pills have appeal for Laotian adoles-cents as a way "to engage in a global youth market, for labourers who seek stamina, [and] for . . . women in the sex industry . . . to converse with prospective customers" (Lyttleton 2006:25). Urine tests with high school students in nine provinces found a jump in ATS use, from 4 per-cent in 2003 to 28 percent in 2005 (Lyttleton 2006). Laotian youth hear that these drugs "create a good mood for hours and should a part-ner be available, [people] can have sex all night" (Lyttleton 2006:25). Prolonged contact of this sort is known to cause breaks in the mucus membrane that facilitate the transmission of HIV and other sexually transmitted diseases.

Drug flows are characterized by three main points along a con-tinuum: countries of production, countries of transshipment, and countries of targeted consumption. For illegal drugs, developing countries are concentrated on the production and transshipment end of this continuum, while legal drugs tend to flow in the opposite direction. In recent years, for example, the former West African Portuguese colony of Guinea-Bissau, a small country wedged between Senegal and Guinea on the Atlantic coast, has become a transshipment site for cocaine from the Andean region of South America on its way to the cities of Europe. Guinea-Bissau is the fifth poorest nation in the world, with an annual per capita income of under $900 and all of the worst indicators of underdevelopment, from a high infant mortality rate to a low life expectancy. As a result of national impoverization, the country has little governmental infrastructure and an unguarded coast comprised of a labyrinth of islands and inlets, making it of great appeal to drug smugglers. As a result, it is estimated that as much as 800 kilograms of cocaine arrive on the coast of Guinea-Bissau every night, part of the 300 tons of cocaine that are thought to be trafficked each year through West African nations to Spain and Portugal, and from there to the other countries of the European Union. According to Aladje Baldé, head of the nongovernmental organization Plan International in Guinea-Bissau, "drug traffickers found an ideal spot to transport drugs to Europe, using Guinea-Bissau as a springboard. . . . [The operations] involved many foreigners who live here; Latin Americans, especially Colombians, have a strong presence here, that has increased markedly over the past year" (quoted in de Queiroz 2007).

Typically, transshipment countries tend to develop their own problems as drugs become available and are adopted among local consumers. As Karan Sharma, deputy director of the Narcotics Control Board, has pointed out with reference to India:

> While India has traditionally been used as a transit country by smugglers of southwest Asian heroin, during the past year, a number of makeshift clandestine heroin laboratories have been detected . . . in the country. The illicitly manufactured heroin might have been intended for use within India. (quoted in *The Times* of India 2001:1)

Often people in transshipment sites have little experience with illicit drugs and no idea how dangerous or addictive they can be, as seen below in an examination of Tajikistan, a place known among travelers as "the roof of the world."

Tajikistan: A Case Study of a Drug Transshipment Country

Tajikistan is a very mountainous, landlocked nation in central Asia, located just north of Afghanistan. It ranks among the 20 poorest countries in the world. Indeed, the Brussels-based International Crisis Group (ICG) suggests that Tajikistan is "threatening to become one of the very few countries where children will lag behind their parents in education" (quoted in Central Eurasia Project 2003). According to the ICG, the Tajikistan agricultural sector does not produce enough food to meet its population's needs and many Tajiks live on about $7–10 per month, or the equivalent of the cost of a single lunch in developed nations. It is estimated that about 65 percent of the population live in abject poverty. At the same time, government revenues are shrinking rapidly.

In the recent period, Tajikistan has been used as an important corridor for heroin from Afghanistan intended for European and Russian markets. As tends to happen with transshipment countries, by 2002, the *United Nations Office for Drug Control and Crime Prevention* (2003) estimated that there were 900 heroin users per 100,000 population in Tajikistan (compared to 600 per 100,000 in Europe). In nearby countries, rates were even higher, with 1,600 users per 100,000 population in Kyrgyzstan and 1,100 users per 100,000 users in Kazakhstan. In addition to being on the heroin corridor, in the words of one Tajik youth who became addicted to heroin in the aftermath of structural adjustment: "It was very prestigious, we saw drugs in movies" (quoted in Shishkin and Crawford 2006). To this youth, like so many others in developing countries who have become addicted to heroin along its pathway to the high-paying markets in Europe, heroin represents nothing like the dark stereotypes that shape its image in the West's long-fought War on Drugs. Instead, for these adolescents and young adults it represents modernity, a point of contact with the valued West. Moreover, the drug is readily available. Another Tajik youth told Davis (2000)

> You only have to ask a couple of your friends and they know where you can go. . . . It's very popular and widespread in [the capital city of] Dushanbe. . . . In each street you can buy any kind of drug here.

Will Straw (1998), a Canadian who has written about oppositional music genres, like punk rock and gangsta rap, notes that the early vinyl recordings of these rebellious musical forms gained considerable worth in the eyes of enthusiastic Canadian consumers because of their origin in Britain or the U.S. Having been transported from the centers of alternative culture and power the records, as things, acquired an aura, the "principal effect [being] to render them cherished and precious." So, too, was heroin in the eyes of the Tajik youth quoted above and among his peers in Tajikistan, and far beyond. Although produced in nearby Afghanistan, heroin possessed the aura of the West, a glittery place, as seen on the "silver screen," of fancy cars, enormous homes, an endless supply of electronic gadgets, food aplenty, and, perhaps most important of all, glamour and prestige. In injecting heroin, this individual like so many of his peers was not taking an illegal drug, he was participating in a world he had come to venerate but that he had little other means of entering. Drugs looked to him not like a dead end but a doorway to the promised land.

Under these difficult circumstances, the ICG points out that drug trafficking

> undermines the political will for economic reform and corrupts government institutions. The drug trade impedes economic growth because this illegal income is rarely transformed into productive capital investments which are necessary for long-term and sustained economic expansion. (quoted in Central Eurasia Project 2003)

The corrupting effects of the drug trade are seen in the arrest in 2000 of Tajikistan's ambassador to Kazakhstan. At the time of his arrest, the ambassador was in possession of 62 kilograms of heroin. Subsequently, the former head of the country's Drug Control Agency was also arrested. On April 11, 2001, Tajikistan Deputy Interior Minister Khabib Sanginov was the victim of a gangland-style murder by as many as eight gunmen, an event that was seen as a sign of intensifying competition among Tajikistan's illicit drug corporations.

Further, the drug trade lures "large numbers of impoverished Tajiks into criminal activity, while fostering health-related problems—in particular, facilitating the spread of HIV/AIDS" (Central Eurasia Project 2003). Finally, drug trafficking may lead to a loss of a significant source of income for almost a million Tajiks, namely migrant laborers in Russia. Remittances from guest workers are estimated to be over $500 million a year, and comprise a significant part of the economy. To block the flow of drugs, however, Russia and other countries are considering closing their borders to Tajik migrant laborers. Given its geographic location, longer-term and recent social history (especially the civil war in 1992–97, which badly damaged the already weak economic infrastructure and caused a painful drop in industrial and agricultural production), political economy, and socioeconomic status, Tajikistan possesses limited internal resources to resist illegal drug flows (Calvani et al. 1997), with a resulting drag on the country's already weak development capacity. As the Silk Road Studies Program of Sweden's Uppsala University (2004) points out:

> Many analysts believe that influential figures from both sides of the [Tajikistan] civil war, many of whom hold positions in the government today, are now involved in the drug trade. . . . While involvement in drug trafficking provides such huge profits and power, the ability of the government to address social problems—drug-related or otherwise—is crippled. Moreover, as politics is privatized into a self-interested profession, the desire to implement development programs is lessened.

GLOBAL TRENDS IN CONTEMPORARY DRUG USE

Legal Drug Use Trends

Products manufactured and distributed internationally by the global tobacco and alcohol industries have caused significant health problems in developing nations. The greatest harm is associated with tobacco products and, thus, it is the tobacco industry that will be the primary focus here. As Barnet and Cavanagh (1994:184) aptly observe, "The cigarette is the most widely distributed global consumer product on earth, the most profitable, and the most deadly." Philip Morris International, for example, has 50 tobacco product factories around the world and sells the commodities they produce in over 160 national markets. Notably, in 2006, U.S. District Judge Gladys Kessler ordered tobacco companies to stop using meaningless terms like "light" and "low tar" to describe their products because the cigarettes that carry these labels are no less harmful than any others. Within two weeks of this ruling, several tobacco companies filed a motion requesting that they be allowed to continue using the terms "light" and "low tar" in overseas cigarette advertising (Arias 2006).

As a result of such tactics, worldwide tobacco consumption is increasing at the rate of one percent per year, with sales in developing nations rising three times faster than in developed countries. With such widespread and growing distribution of such a dangerous product it is not surprising that tobacco-related diseases are the leading cause of death in developing countries (Stebbins 1990, 2001). Moreover, as Nichter and Cartwright (1991) stress, smoking damages the health and well-being of families in the developing world in several ways: by exacerbating chronic diseases among working adults, by reducing the ability of adults to care for children, by exposing children to toxic substances through passive smoking, and by diverting scarce resources into nonproductive uses.

While the tobacco industry, traditionally, had a free hand in advertising and promoting its products around the world, in recent years, as the knowledge of the deadly nature of smoking has diffused widely, developing nations have begun to enact laws to restrict advertising and other forms of promotion by the tobacco industry. In response, transnational tobacco companies have shown that they are not adverse to bending or outright breaking the law. A case in point can be found on the island nation of Mauritius, which lies in the Indian Ocean east of Madagascar.

In 1999 the government of Mauritius joined the swelling ranks of countries trying to put the brakes on aggressive promotion of tobacco consumption by modifying the nation's Public Health Act to ban tobacco advertising and specifying that "no person involved in the production, marketing, distribution or sale of any tobacco product shall offer, or agree to provide, any form of sponsorship to any other person in relation to a tobacco product or trade name or brand associated with a tobacco product" (quoted in LeClézio 2002). According to the Mauritian antismoking group, ViSa, the British American Tobacco company (BAT), which has included Mauritius as a market since 1926, reacted to the amended law and ban on tobacco company sponsorships through an aggressive if veiled promotional effort that included: (1) donating libraries to poorer villages, with the support of national government officials, and promoting the opening of these libraries and other resources through media photographs and reports that mentioned the company name; (2) donating prenatal and orthopedic wards to Mauritian public hospitals; (3) sponsoring a national art gallery; (4) building a home for elderly people; (5) advertising smoking products through the use of help-wanted notices in local newspapers; (6) using youth smoking prevention programs at point of purchase sites to draw customer attention to cigarette displays; (7) giving away T-shirts displaying the company's logo to all of the walkers at the annual Day of the Blind fund-raiser; (8) instituting the competitive BAT Undergraduate Scholarship program and organizing free training opportunities for students at BAT Mauritius; and (9) developing youth smoking prevention materials that portray tobacco products as an adult reward, thereby making use of them a marker of grown-up status (LeClézio 2002). Not only was BAT not prosecuted for violating Mauritius' Public Health Act, ironically, given the nature of its business, in 2001 BAT was awarded the first prize in the National Occupational Health and Safety competition held jointly by the Mauritius Ministry of Health and Ministry of Labour.

As countries around the globe also have begun to enact laws to restrict the advertising of tobacco products to children, tobacco companies, although they deny that they are attempting to market cigarettes or other tobacco products to underage customers, have nonetheless engaged in an array of strategies that appear to be designed to circumvent national laws and gain new waves of youthful adherents (Global Partnerships for Tobacco Control 2002), including: (1) in Togo, where youth numerically dominate the population and soccer is king, tobacco products are linked through advertisements to music and soccer, and such "[a]dvertising and marketing continues to be conducted aggressively and in contempt of existing laws" (Agbavon 2001); (2) in Uruguay, Philip Morris carried out a promotional campaign entitled "Yo tengo poder" ("I have the power") that was specifically directed to children in public schools; and (3) in Jordan, girls dressed in red visit restaurants and give away free cigarettes, 10 packs of Marlboros per person, smokers and nonsmokers alike. Similar youth-oriented strategies are used by tobacco companies in many other developing countries, suggesting a systematic global program for the development of a new generation of addicted smokers. As Seabrook (1999) observes, "It is an epic irony that tobacco, a product of Empire, should now be pushed most vigorously by colonising tobacco companies to those who have supposedly freed themselves from the colonial yoke."

As these examples suggest, the tobacco industry has long known that passing laws is one thing, enforcing them is another. In resource-poor and developing countries, in particular, bountiful tobacco profits can be used in a wide variety of ways to gain a considerable amount of influence and to successfully promote smoking among selected target audiences. In light of the impact of the tobacco industry on the lives of children worldwide, Nichter and Cartwright (1991) have questioned whether all of the global public health and development efforts that have been carried out to insure child survival (e.g., mass immunization, oral rehydration campaigns to combat diarrheal disease) may be undone by the war for drug use waged by the tobacco industry. They question if we are "saving the children for the tobacco industry." The tobacco companies, in short, have their own millennial development goals and they contradict and undermine those of that have been embraced by developing nations.

In some instances, countries have enacted laws restricting the import of foreign-made tobacco products in an effort to protect their local tobacco production. In response, major tobacco companies have resorted to tobacco smuggling. Analyses of these smuggling efforts suggest that they are designed to gain a foothold in restricted markets and by doing so weaken local producers. In this way, "tobacco companies . . . use the smuggling problem as a bargaining chip to convince governments to lower tariffs" (Zill 2002). According to a long-time cigarette smuggler interviewed by the Center for Public Integrity, "It's very clear to me that tobacco companies knew more about smuggling and how it worked and how to improve it than any smugglers on Earth" (quoted in Center for Public Integrity 2001). Moreover, there is considerable evidence, that these smuggling activities put tobacco companies in direct collaboration with underground criminal groups engaged in moving large quantities of cigarettes across national boundaries. According to Douglas Tweddle, the former director for compliance and facilitation of the Brussels-based World Customs Organization, an independent intergovernmental body concerned with international custom laws, "Organized criminals, who have traditionally been involved in smuggling illicit narcotics, are suddenly realizing that tobacco is a good thing to get into, as you make just as much money, and it's perhaps not quite as anti-social" (quoted in Center for Public Integrity 2001).

In order to limit the significant cost of tobacco promotion and use on the health and well-being of the world's population, in 2000 the World Health Organization, led by a block of all 46 African nations, began negotiating an international treaty called the Framework Convention on Tobacco Control (FCTC). The goal of the FCTC is changing the way the tobacco industry operates, including imposing significant restrictions on advertising, promotion, and sponsorship; excluding the tobacco industry from having a role in the formation of public health policy; and establishing in international law the consumer's right to know about the dangers of tobacco use. Internal documents from Philip Morris/Altria reveal the response of the tobacco industry to the FCTC, namely the implementation of a strategy that emphasizes: "The first alternative to an onerous convention is to delay its crafting and adoption. . . ." (quoted in Global Health Watch 2006:311), while recommending specific points in the adoption of the FCTC at which delaying tactics could be used. Nonetheless, the treaty became the law in ratifying countries on February 27, 2005. During the period between the first negotiation of the FCTC and its ratification, 20 million people died of tobacco-related diseases.

Illegal Drug Use Trends

Although methods have improved, estimating the production, trafficking and consumption of illicit drugs in developing countries remains a highly problematic endeavor given limitations on data collection. It is known that patterns of drug use in developing nations vary by drug and by region (UN Office on Drugs and Crime 2003). While various drug control mechanisms have been establhed over the years (see chapter 4), analysis of recent trends "makes quite gloomy reading for those hoping to see elimination or significant reduction: the overriding impression is one of stable or increasing trends at the global level in recent years. However, this stability masks dynamic changes at the national and regional level" (Forward Thinking on Drug Use 2003).

With regard to opiate use, for example, it is evident that there has been a shift in the center of production from Southeast to Southwest Asia. While there has been a general decline over the last decade in opium production in the traditional Golden Triangle area in countries like Myanmar and Lao PDR, between 1998 and 2002 there was a 16 percent increase in Southwest Asia. The notably productive irrigated opium fields of Afghanistan, coupled with the removal of the Taliban government by the U.S. and the resulting breakdown in government control outside of the capital, have led to an increasing concentration of global opium production in that country.

In 2006, the United Nations Office of Drugs and Crime and the World Bank issued a joint report entitled *Afghanistan's Drug Industry: Structure, Functioning, Dynamics, and Implications for Counter-Nar-*

cotics Policy. A primary conclusion of the report was that efforts to combat opium production in Afghanistan have very limited success and have been significantly weakened by corruption. The wealthiest opium producers have been able to pay bribes to national, regional, or local government officials to protect their fields from eradication efforts, a process that has undermined the credibility of the government and its local representatives. According to the UN report, police chiefs, governors, and other government officials profit from the drug trade. Consequently, eradication has targeted smaller-scale and poorer opium farmers who are unable to pay bribes. Far from leading to sustained general declines in the total cultivation of opium poppy, success in reducing cultivation in one province has only led to increases in production in others. Consequently, in 2006 there was a record opium harvest, with total cultivation of opium poppy increasing by 59 percent and production of raw opium increasing by 49 percent. The UN found that the amount of land devoted to growing poppies in Afghanistan jumped to over 400,000 acres in 2006 compared to about 255,000 acres in 2005. As a result, in 2006 Afghanistan accounted for more than 90 percent of global illegal opium production, and the opium economy comprised about one-third of the total economy of the country.

Most opiate users (about half of the world's total) are found in Asia, especially in and around Afghanistan and Myanmar. The highest prevalence rates per capita are in Iran, the Lao PDR, and Kyrgyzstan. The overall largest number of opiate users, however, is found in India, although prevalence in India is lower than in neighboring Pakistan or Myanmar. While overall levels of opiate use in Latin America are low compared to Asia, the emergence of heroin production in several South American countries has resulted in increasing prevalence of use in Colombia, Venezuela, Panama, Chile, and Argentina. While generally low, opiate use has been rising in Africa, with strongest increases in Namibia and Zimbabwe.

By contrast, in the developing world, cocaine use is most concentrated in Latin America and the Caribbean, but there has been increased use in recent years in western (e.g., Benin, Gambia, Ghana, and Togo) and southern Africa (Zimbabwe). Levels of cocaine use remain low in Asia, but there has been increasing use in parts of the Middle East. Some of the most dramatic increases in drug use in developing nations in recent years have involved amphetamine-type stimulants (ATS), including amphetamine, methamphetamine, and, although different in its effects, ecstasy. Between 1992 and 2001, the number of countries reporting increased ATS abuse tripled. In several countries in East and Southeast Asia, especially Thailand and the Philippines, methamphetamine has become the main drug of abuse. Thailand, in fact, has developed one of the highest per capita methamphetamine prevalence rates worldwide. The Philippines is another growing methamphetamine market and estimates suggest that drug abuse, in general, and the abuse of methamphetamine in particular, increased from negligible levels during the 1970s to high levels during the 1990s. Relatively high levels of ATS consumption also have emerged in several countries in South America and in Africa.

Beyond the opiates, cocaine, and ATS, an array of other drugs continues to spread among developing countries, contributing to an overall increase in levels of use. Some of these, like inhalants, are particularly common among younger users. In countries like Brazil and Mexico, for example, solvents rank second after marijuana in prevalence of use among children and involve 5–10 percent of children less than 18 years of age (UN Office on Drugs and Crime 1994).

An important issue in the assessment of global illicit drug trends is that of *drug use dynamics*, that is, the tendency for constant change in the social domain of drug use (Singer 2006b). Change occurs in many ways in the world of drug use, and changes that emerge in one local community may quickly or slowly diffuse to others or nationally and even globally. Some of the primary kinds of change include: (1) the introduction of new drugs, such as ecstasy (MDMA) in the 1970s, and their subsequent rapid global diffusion (both in terms of manufacture and consumption); (2) the diversion of pharmaceutical medicines to street drug use, such as the emergence of buprenorphine, a pharmaceutical analgesic, as the main injection drug in most of India; (3) the marketing of new forms of older drugs, such as crack cocaine in the Caribbean; (4) the mixing of new drug combinations, such as blending heroin with sedatives like triazolam among injection drug users in China; (5) the adoption of new drug use equipment, such as the worldwide spread of portable plastic diabetic syringes with fixed needles; (6) the discovery of new ways to consume existing drugs, such as alcohol injection in Colombia; (7) the restructuring of drug production processes and distribution patterns leading to changes in drug purity, availability, price, and composition, such as refinements in South American heroin production that led to much purer drug products; and (8) the development of new populations of drug users, such as street youth in many developing countries.

Overall, it is clear that with regard to patterns of drug use "a division is appearing between the fortunes of developed and developing countries. While trends in use in developed countries are largely stabilising or falling, increasing problems are being experienced in developing countries, especially where poverty and ready access to drugs of addiction collide" (Forward Thinking on Drug Use 2003).

Drugs commodities have spread widely, with important negative impacts on the health and well-being of societies, including functioning as a barrier to economic and social development and to the achievement of human dignity. These issues are addressed in chapter 3.

Chapter Three

The Impacts of Drugs on Development

Coastline of Guinea-Bissau. (Photo by Margaret L. Buckner)

COMPLEXITIES OF DRUGS AND DEVELOPMENT

Assessing the role of drugs in underdevelopment is not an easy or straightforward task. Indeed, it is fair to say that drugs pose a paradox for development initiatives. In the introduction to their edited volume *Drug Use and Cultural Contexts 'Beyond the West,'* for example, British sociologists Ross Coomber and Nigel South stress that there are many forms of drug use "that simply 'do not fit' the supposedly progressive, western notion of all drug use as essentially damaging" (2004:16). Rather, they argue, there are numerous examples from around the world that are best understood as representing "positive, integrative and functional contributions of drug use to the social-health of particular communities of people," a point that has long been emphasized with reference to indigenous patterns of alcohol consumption by American anthropologist Dwight Heath, based on his research among the Camba of Bolivia (1958, 1991).

Ganguly (2004:83) observes that in large areas of rural India opium "is used in ways that signify both the importance of its use to individuals and communities as well as the normality of its use, in the sense that it is highly integrated into the everyday fabric of communities." Rather than being disruptive and damaging, in these communities, opium use facilitates social gatherings, enhances social interactions, reinforces group customs and traditional norms, and helps sustain community social institutions. This pattern is not unique to rural India but rather is fairly common for a variety of drugs in diverse social settings. In these places, informal social constraints on the amount, duration, and contexts of use are in place, as is cultural knowledge about how to behave while under the influence. As a result, drug use tends not to fit the Western view that such behavior in all places and at all times destroys lives and communities.

Drugs and Income

Moreover, stemming from the fact that involvement in drug production, transport, and sales provides income for many poor individuals and families with limited access to alternative sources of cash, drugs in certain contexts may be a critical economic asset. As the United Nations Office on Drugs and Crime (1994:1) has noted, "Despite its illegality, the drug trade in some cases provides the basic necessities for economic survival. And that is the point at which the interests of people in the fields of drug control and development intersect." Opium, for example, is the biggest employer in Afghanistan (Barker 2006). Elsewhere, as well, where opium poppies and the latex they produce (i.e., raw opium) bring a higher price than other crops, drugs are vital source of income among the rural poor. For people like Fernay Lugo and Blanca Ruby Pérez, two Colombian peasant farmers interviewed by *New York Times* reporters Juan Forero and Tim Weiner (2002:1), poppies provide a means of survival in a world of threatening hunger and financial ruin:

> Here in rugged southern Colombia, a one-acre plot belongs to
> Fernay Lugo, rail thin and agile, who works, razor in hand, slicing

open the pods of his blossoming poppies to collect the milky gum that is refined into heroin. He explained how—day after day, bit by bit, in mountains 7,000 feet up—he tries to accumulate a few pounds, enough to sell for the kind of profits his slumping coffee plants could never fetch. He does not ponder who his buyers are, the shadowy men who meet him at a distant roadside, or their ultimate customers. "When we harvest and sell, we do not even think where it goes," said Mr. Lugo, 29, the father of two girls. . . . Farmers also disperse their poppy crops, Mr. Lugo said, to make them harder to identify by satellite and reconnaissance aircraft. . . . Blanca Ruby Pérez, 39, said she and her family lived by poppies, which can be harvested twice a year and bring far more money than blackberries, corn, beans and lettuce. "It is much easier to grow than the other crops," she said, carefully tiptoeing around the small, green leaves. "Look, we have put no fertilizer on it, and look how pretty it is."

Similarly, among poor farming families in Myanmar, Grund (2004) notes that growing opium poppies "pays for what most people in developed countries take for granted." In the words of one Myanmar man, "Opium is our food, our clothes, our medicine, the education of our children," (quoted in Grund, 2004:2). Likewise, cocaine production in South America has attracted thousands of families fleeing extreme poverty in other locations to coca-growing regions, coca being perhaps the only cultivated plant they could make a living from in a region in which the soil is not well suited to intensive agriculture. For these families, the "coca option" offers a means of staying a step ahead of household collapse and complete destitution. Notably, one of the important forces pushing the poor to adopt the "coca option" is the structural adjustment policies (SAPs) of neoliberalism:

> In Peru, for instance, the implementation of SAPs has put four million people in extreme poverty, almost halved real wages and cut those with "adequate employment" to 15% of the workforce. Consequently, there has been a forced migration of impoverished peasants and urban unemployed into coca growing as an alternative to starvation. (Ismi 2002)

Drug Development

Additionally, in urban areas of countries heavily involved in drug production, especially in the impoverished communities from which illicit drug capitalists often emerge, public development projects are sometimes paid for with drug profits (E. Arias 2006). For example, when the police in Rio de Janeiro killed Erismar Moreira, the colorful leader of the Amigos dos Amigos (Friends of the Friends), an illicit drug corporation, city officials cheered, but in the squatter community of Rocinha where he lived, black banners were hung in remembrance on the main street and Moreira's initials were spray painted on surrounding walls. It was well-known to community residents that during his brief stint as an illicit drug entrepreneur Moreira used some drug profits to fund soccer fields and sponsor lavish community parties. Also his drug organization is credited by the community with building the water tower that helps insure the steady flow of potable water, a responsibility ignored by city officials. At another of Rio's favelas, Vagário Geral, drug traffickers are credited with maintaining a fresh water system, building homes for residents, bringing in medicines, using their vans to take residents to the hospital, building a soccer field, and maintaining internal security. The traffickers were especially popular with the poorest residents of the community (E. Arias 2006).

In a parallel if even grander example, Clawson and Lee report that illicit cocaine corporations in Colombia have sponsored "some high-profile civic programs, including the donation of several hundred new housing units to poor slum dwellers and construction of some eighty illuminated sports arenas in Medellín and surrounding communities" (1998:48). In Medellín, a center of the Colombian cocaine trade, illicit drug entrepreneur Pablo Escobar developed a local reputation by using drug money to pay for planting trees, building schools, fixing broken sewer lines, developing recreational facilities, and providing bricks for home construction in poor neighborhoods.

The Downside

These illustrations of the fiscal, social, and developmental contributions of the drug trade notwithstanding, there are multiple arenas of negative drug impact on development. Notes the UN Office on Drugs and Crime (1994:3), "Not even the most ardent supporter of laissez-faire economics would argue that the negative impact on health of smoking is somehow outweighed by the employment generated in the tobacco and medical industries. The analogy holds [for] the illicit drug industry." Thus, even in rural India where traditional opium use is widespread and even normative, Ganguly affirms that "a background noise of resentment can be heard and [users are] questioned as to the waste of time and in some cases of precious financial resources due to the use of opium" (2004:95).

Even among the Camba of Bolivia, a group long cited in the literature for their controlled, nonproblematic yet heavy use of alcohol, things have changed. Older ways of life were destroyed as the forests were cut down by the lumber industry, in part to fund large sugar refineries as well as to clear land for large-scale cotton and cattle raising businesses. Many Camba lost their land and customary way of life. At the same time, the traditional Camba economy was "displaced by the illegal trade in coca and cocaine paste" (Heath 2004:132). In other words, while traditional, community-controlled, and socially integrative drug use occurs, it tends to be in settings where the drugs in question are produced for use, not as commodities sold on the market, and where community social life has not been disrupted by the forces of globalization. It is precisely globalization's disruption of social conditions that causes drugs to become a disintegrative force that hinders rather than contributes to social and economic development. As this social distinction should make clear, drugs are not inherently disruptive because of their chemical composition or the considerable impact drug chemistry has on brain functioning, rather they become a threat to human health and society under particular political and economic structural conditions.

It is also noteworthy that analyses by the International Narcotics Control Board (INCB)—an independent body established by the Single Convention on Narcotic Drugs to monitor the compliance of governments with international drug control treaties—indicate the bulk of profits made from illicit drug trafficking is not spent in the Third World countries in which drug crops are grown but in the developed nations in which the final products are often sold and consumed. According to Dr. Philip Emafo, president of the INCB:

> Only one per cent of the money that is ultimately spent by drug abusers is generated as farm income in developing countries. . . . The remaining 99 per cent of global illicit drug income are earned by drug trafficking groups operating at various other points along the drug trafficking chain. (quoted in EuropaWorld 2002)

BARRIERS TO DEVELOPMENT

Drugs have both direct and indirect negative impacts on development, across populations, age groups, institutions, and spheres of life. The five most significant arenas of impact are:

- Damage to productivity
- Threat to youth
- Health consequences
- Corruption and the breakdown of public institutions
- Violence

Each of these impacts on development and their specific and varied expressions in underdeveloped countries are examined below. Notably, some of these factors are of greater importance than others in particular national or even local settings, as is the mixture of negative impacts in any particular setting. Because they often are interconnected, it is not always possible to discuss one of these factors without mention of others, as seen below.

Damage to Productivity

Drugs can have a direct impact on national productivity. This occurs in several ways and includes effects on both the drug supply and consumption.

The Supply Side. There are significant occupational risks faced in the production of drugs. Many of the people who toil in drug labs around the world—daily mixing and pouring the chemicals and managing the processes that turn natural or synthetic substances into powerful psychotropics—are like 18-year-old Nilofar from a small Afghan village (PakTribune 2006). Both of Nilofar's parents are dead, and, after her wedding, her husband died too. With few alternatives, she and her 16-year-old sister went to work in a heroin lab; it was the only work around, the only means of survival they could find. Then she got sick, because of the toxic substances she was exposed to during the process of making the heroin. Her sister got sick as well. In fact, many of the lab workers she knew were suffering from challenging health problems, rashes, asthma, blood deficiencies, diarrhea, and stomach upset.

As generally is the case, the health of workers is a reflection of their social relations with their employers. Workers who have struggled and won rights and concessions from their bosses tend to live and work under healthier conditions than those who have not been able to successfully counter the tendency of employers to increase profits by not protecting workers from occupational or environmental dangers (Levy and Sidel 2006). Working in an illicit trade makes it hard for drug lab workers to organize; certainly it is all but impossible to pressure the government to come to their aid, as is sometimes possible in legal industries. As a result, they are at the mercy of their bosses, and their subordinate social position may literally be etched in their bodies in the illnesses they suffer from the kinds of work they do in illicit drug production.

The risk to workers in illicit production is enhanced with the spread of ATS in developing countries. In the production of drugs like methamphetamine extremely dangerous toxins, like phosphine, are released. Additionally, explosions and fires are fairly common in illicit methamphetamine labs because of the volatile chemicals in use and the makeshift operating conditions. A growing number of ATS labs are being discovered in developing countries. From 1997 to 2004, for example, 32 labs were discovered and dismantled by the police in the Philippines (Devaney, Reid, and Baldwin 2005). This shift to local production is facilitated by the spread of knowledge and relative simplicity of transforming precursor drugs like ephedrine into methamphetamine.

Also on the supply side, low-level workers and transporters in the drug trade are the most likely to be detected and arrested. For example, from the lab where Nilofar works, processed heroin must be bagged in small quantities and transported, usually through a circuitous route, often through various middlemen, to the market. Nilofar was one of those who briefly played a role in this process. Seeking to raise the money needed to see a doctor, she agreed to transport processed heroin to India. But, like many others at her level at the bottom of the illicit transport system, she was caught in the Kabul airport and taken to prison. This pattern is found throughout the developing world. In Jakarta, Indonesia, for example, the police reported 4,799 drug-related arrests in 2003, a 39 percent increase from the year before. Most of those arrested were 19–30 years of age, prime production years, and 283 were 10–18 years old. Nationally, the number of drug arrests increased approximately 58 percent a year from 1999 to 2004. Similarly, in Malaysia, which has declared drugs to be "public enemy number one," the government reported a substantial increase in drug-related incarcerations for 1996–2002 (Devaney, Reid, and Baldwin 2005). Rising rates of drug-related arrests, primarily of "drug mules" caught transporting small quantities of drugs in the service of major drug corporations, and lower-level dealers and users, can be found throughout the developing world. These countries are often pressured by the U.S. and other developed countries and their lending institutions to mount local wars on drugs, and rising arrest rates can serve as empirical evidence of compliance with such dictates.

The Use Side.   It is generally recognized that

> productivity gains are crucial for a country's competitive position in the world marketplace. The dynamics of the problem come even more sharply into focus when it is recognized that some developing countries are outpacing developed countries in rates of drug addiction. Thirty years ago in Pakistan, for example, the number of drug addicts was negligible. . . . Ten years ago there were approximately 30,000 heroin addicts. Today there are approximately 1.5 million. (United Nations Office on Drugs and Crime 1994:5)

Drug use can lower productivity through occupational injuries, the spread of diseases, and drug overdoses. Drug use has been found to be particularly widespread in certain work sectors in the developing world. In the jade mines of Myanmar, for example, nearly all male workers, a group that constitutes the majority of miners, have been found to be heroin users (Scott-Clark and Levy 2002). Mining is also linked to drug use, especially alcohol consumption (as well as commercial sex and the spread of HIV/AIDS), in South Africa. There mine workers must migrate far from their homes, live in all-male labor camps or hostels, and turn to intoxication to cope with oppressive living and working conditions. The spread of drugs among workers has been linked to an increase in occupational accidents and absenteeism.

An International Labor Organization (ILO) (1994) study in Egypt, Mexico, Namibia, Poland, and Sri Lanka, for example, found that users have 2–4 times more accidents on the job than other workers and are absent 2–3 times more often. As noted below, drug use has been a major factor in the spread of HIV/AIDS in developing countries, often as a result of syringe sharing and reuse. Drug overdoses also have been rising in developing nations as new drugs are introduced to inexperienced users. Overall, the effects of substance abuse on national productivity are significant.

The Threat to Youth

Youth and emergent adults have proven to be particularly at risk from involvement in drugs, both as consumers and as a source of disposable labor for drug trafficking groups. According to World Bank data, illicit drug users in developing countries "typically fall within the age group of 15–44, although most are in their mid-twenties. In Latin America, drug use tends to begin at younger ages with use especially common in 12–22 year olds" (1993:89). As noted by the United Nations Office on Drugs and Crime (1994:3) "drug abuse often attacks people during their most productive years, thereby converting a vibrant source of productivity into a burden on society. Particularly prevalent among younger individuals is the deliberate inhalation of solvents and various commercial aerosols." Children and adolescents have easy access to solvents such as glue, aerosols, thinners, gasoline, and paint, as these substances are readily available, are of relatively low cost, and produce a powerful psychotropic effect. Use of solvents by street children is widespread in Latin America, Africa, and central and eastern Europe.

As a result of widespread poverty, urban migration, and breakdowns in the social service sector following structural adjustment, many cities in the developing world, from Mongolia to India to Brazil, have large numbers of homeless children. India, for example, has a significant population of homeless youth living in cities like Mumbai, Kolkata, and New Delhi; it is estimated that there are over 100,000 street children in these cities, and many are involved in solvent or other drug use (United Nations Development Programme 1993). For these youth, sale of illicit drugs may offer a means of survival in a hostile, unsupportive social environment, as well as a source of peer respectability and acceptance and a temporary escape from a harsh reality that entails a risky lifestyle and frequent potential for victimization. In recent years, similar patterns have developed in Southeast Asia and Cambodia. Laos and Vietnam now have "substantial populations of street children [involved in] consuming drugs, living precariously with little or no family support or guardians" (Devaney, Reid, and Baldwin 2005:xiii). These homeless children receive no education or training that would allow them to participate in national development.

The International Labor Organization, a body of the United Nations, estimates that as many as 250 million children between 5 and 14 years of age are economically active around the world (de Souza and Urani 2002). The use of children in the production and trafficking of drugs, as well as in other and often related illicit activities (e.g., commercial sex), is broadly recognized in the international community as one of the most exploitive expressions of child labor. Research on the involvement of youth in the drug trade suggests significant consequences for both the youth and the wider society. De Souza and Urani (2002), for example, have used rapid assessment techniques to examine the involvement of children and adolescents in drug trafficking in Rio de Janeiro, Brazil. They found that youth involved in the drug trade often come from the poorest families, including many from the densely crowded shantytown slums or favelas that occupy many of the hillsides around the city. These youth have comparatively limited education relative to other youth in the city.

Young people become involved in drug trafficking because of a lack of alternative ways to make a living and survive and because of the prestige, a sense of power (expressed through purchasing of valued consumer goods and brandishing firearms), excitement, and adventure associated with illicit activities. Their primary friendships are with other youth involved in drug trafficking, and their bonds with other youth in the drug trade contribute to continued involvement over time. Another factor is that after a while the identities of these youth become known to rival drug groups as well as the police, making it difficult to leave their protective drug social networks. The greatest fear expressed by the youth in the ILO study was of imprisonment, death, and betrayal by their friends. Many of the youth hope that through their participation in drug distribution and sales they will be able to acquire enough money to move out of the favelas, although few of them are able to build up any cash reserves, as saving money contradicts the fast-paced lifestyle of the drug world.

De Souza and Urani found that the youth they studied focus on acquiring status symbols as a reflection of their involvement in the wider, corporate-driven consumer culture that fuels globalization.

> In a consumer society that confers more importance to what one "possesses" than to who one "is," clothes or the equivalent products acquire new meaning. They become a symbol of power and belonging. They represent an important form of distinction, as defined by Pierre Bourdieu. . . . The illusion of consumption imparts to these teenagers a sensation of strength; they possess something that inequality, intrinsic to Brazilian society, limits. (de Souza and Urani 2002:13)

Adds Moreira (2000:109), "It is so important and gratifying for them to enter a clothes shop in a shopping center, choose the clothes that they like most, try them on and buy them, that it justifies the risks of working in drug traffic." Notably, de Souza and Urani (2002) found that the age of entry into drug trafficking groups has been falling, going from age 15–16 during the 1990s to 12–13 by the year 2000.

CORRUPTION AND THE BREAKDOWN OF SOCIAL INSTITUTIONS

Pablo Escobar, a key figure in the Colombian illicit cocaine trade during the 1980s, implemented an approach he called *placa o plomo* (silver or lead) in which government officials were given a choice between accepting a bribe or facing assassination (Singer 2007). While some individuals resisted, and several were killed by Escobar's soldiers, many accepted placa over plomo. This example illustrates one aspect of the corrupting effects of drugs, a pattern that can significantly undercut development efforts.

In this regard, the German organization, Transparency International, has developed a gauge called the Corruption Perceptions Index (CPI) to measure the perceived corruption in a country—defined as abuse of public office for private gain. The CPI is a composite index based on expert opinion surveys of public-sector corruption. Transparency International uses this approach because it is well-known that hard empirical data on the amount of bribes or the number of prosecutions or court cases are either all but impossible to come by or they do not reveal the extent of corruption but only government capacity to stop it. The CPI scores countries on a scale from zero to ten, with zero indicating high levels of perceived corruption and ten indicating low levels of perceived corruption. In 2006, Transparency International released a report on levels of corruption in over 160 countries. The report gives Guyana, for example, a CPI of 2.5, making it the second highest to Haiti in the greater Caribbean region in terms of perceived level of corruption. Notably, almost "three-quarters of the countries [included] in the CPI score below five, including all low-income countries, and all but two African states, indicating that most countries in the world face serious perceived levels of domestic corruption" (French 2006). Transparency International also reports a direct correlation between level of perceived corruption and the extent of poverty in a nation, as poverty and corruption often go hand in hand.

Officials on the Take

In the mid-1990s, Colombian President Ernesto Samper was charged with using over $3 million of illicit drug money in his election campaign, his defense minister, Feranando Botero Zea, was convicted of accepting and using drug money during the campaign, and his campaign treasurer, Santiago Medina, was accused of seeking large campaign contributions from the cocaine capitalists in the city of Cali. Additionally, nine members of the Colombian Congress were publicly linked to the underground drug trade. In South America, but in many other regions of the world as well, in underdeveloped and developed countries alike, drug trafficking has contributed to the weakening of key social institutions, with telling effects throughout society.

A particularly well-documented example of drug-related corruption among government officials is found in the case of the Bahamas in the period from 1978 to 1982. It was during these years that the Colombian cocaine trafficker, Carlos Lehder, a confederate of Escobar, based his operation on a small Bahamian island called Norman's Cay. Lehder developed close relations with members of the Bahamian government, and, in exchange for a considerable amount of money, they provided Lehder with protection to coordinate his vast drug business from the island nation. According to one of Lehder's associates, Carlos Toros:

> He operated on the island from the beginning because he had the blessing of the Bahamian government. They were funneling tons of money.... The Bahamian government gave Carlos a promise. We will advise you. You will get a wink from us, a signal, when things are getting too hot and you need to move out of there. (*FRONTLINE* 2000)

This is precisely what came to pass, but Lehder did not escape arrest for very long. After Lehder was behind bars, a Commission of Inquiry was established and in 1984 issued a 500-page report that revealed the extent of drug corruption within the Bahamian government, as well as the range of social problems on the island caused by the cocaine trade (Smith 2006). In response to the report, Deputy Prime Minister Arthur Hanna called on the prime minister to resign. According to Kendal Issacs, a leader of the Free National Movement party, "The greatest shocks we have had to suffer in 1984 have been the twin revelations of epidemic drug use among our people, and the incredible corruption in the PLP [Progressive Liberal Party] as a government and as a party" (quoted in Smith 2006). The Commission of Inquiry's review of the prime minister's personal finances found that he spent eight times his reported income for the period from 1977 to 1984, and that over $50 million he possessed could not be accounted for through reported income. In the commission's report a cabinet minister, senior police officers, and high-level officers in the Royal Bahamas Defense Force were exposed as having taken bribes from Lehder and were forced to resign. Further, a number of prominent lawyers were found to be the go-betweens in bribing public officials. A cabinet minister and judge, as well as several members of Parliament, also were found to have accepted bribes. According to the commission's report:

> We were alarmed by the extent to which persons in the public ser-
> vice have been corrupted by money derived from the illegal drug
> trade. . . . We were particularly concerned to discover that these cor-
> rupting influences made their presence felt at the level of perma-
> nent secretary and minister. (Commission of Inquiry 1984:8)

As a result of the use of the Bahamas for cocaine reshipment, a
significant drug problem developed on the island nation, as did a rising crime rate. These problems were fueled as well by a high rate of
unemployment, especially among teenagers and young adults. In 1986
the Bahamas National Task Force against Drugs reported that domestic drug abuse and addiction had reached epidemic proportions (Neville and Clark 1985).

In more recent years, countries in West Africa, such as Guinea-
Bissau, which as noted previously have become key transit points for
cocaine traffickers, have begun to show the consequences of playing
this role in the international drug trade. One of the largest cocaine seizures in Guinea-Bissau occurred on September 26, 2006, when police
in the capital arrested two men with Venezuelan passports who were in
possession of 675 kilograms of cocaine. The local value of the seized
cocaine can seen by noting that an average year's income in the country
is equivalent to the monetary value of just six grams of cocaine, while
the total annual budget of the government of Guinea-Bissau is about
equal to the wholesale value of 2,200 kilograms of cocaine in Europe.

The confiscated drugs were locked in a safe in the national trea-
sury but soon disappeared. They were taken by men in army uniforms
who reported they had to weigh the drugs. While the army denied
involvement, the cash-strapped government is unable to regularly pay
police or soldiers or provide the severance packages to retirees promised when they enlisted. According to the country's minister of justice,
Namuano Gomes:

> How do they expect policemen who are not getting paid to hand in
> bags of drugs and receive nothing in return? How do they expect
> civilians to come forward with information when we can offer them
> no incentives and when people at all levels of society are profiting
> by facilitating the drug trade? (quoted in Worldpress.org 2007:1)

Subsequently, in a speech before the Security Council of the United
Nations, Antonio Maria Costa of the Office on Drugs and Crime (2007a:1)
reported that "[u]sing threats and bribes, drug traffickers are infiltrating
state structures [in Guinea-Bissau] and operating with impunity." In a
report on the West Africa's vulnerability to corruption, Costa's program
notes, "Once a critical mass of law enforcement is taking bribes, it may
become difficult, or even dangerous to remain honest. In a vicious cycle,
citizen cooperation declines with each police failure, further undermining
the ability of officials to do their jobs" (Destrebecq and Leggett 2007:11).

Drug-related corruption, in sum, has several faces. It not only involves the bribing of government officials to turn a blind eye to drug-related activities or to actively aid them, it also involves ensnaring law enforcement representatives to provide cover for the movement and street sales of illicit substances. Moreover, police and other members of law enforcement engage in selling off confiscated drugs while court officials take bribes to destroy records of drug seizures.

Market seller in Guinea-Bissau. (Photo by Brandon Lundy)

Legal Drugs and Corruption

While the extent of drug-related corruption in the Bahamas was extensive, similar patterns have been recorded in other developing countries as well. Notably, not all of the corruption is the result of trafficking of illicit drugs like cocaine and heroin but involves legally manufactured drugs as well. In 1995, for example, distributors for Philip Morris cigarettes were indicted for laundering $40 million in what the government called a "black market peso" operation involving purchase of Philip Morris products for illegal sale in Colombia. Five years later when Philip Morris was sued by a group of Colombian tax collectors who accused the company of involvement in cigarette smuggling and drug money laundering, the company, without admitting to wrongdoing, agreed to prevent its products from entering the black market or being used in money laundering (Zill and Bergman 2001).

The Family

Another social institution that is put at risk by drugs is the family. Typical is the family of Georgette, a struggling Jamaican woman in her late 30s, which was torn apart by her involvement in the drug trade. A single mother anxious to find money to support her children and unable to pay her water, electric, and other bills, she could not resist the many offers made from local drug dealers in her neighborhood for "fast cash." Consequently, in April of 2002, she boarded a plane in Kingston, Jamaica, headed for London; with her was a suitcase filled with cocaine. The morning she left, she reported, "was my son's eighth birthday. . . . I remember that my little girl was crying and I kissed her and told her I'd be back in three weeks' time. I did feel bad but at the end of the day I needed the money" (quoted in Ash 2006). Caught at Heathrow Airport in possession of drugs, she instead spent four years in prison in Morton Hall in Lincolnshire, England, before being able to return to Jamaica. She was not the lone Jamaican "drug mule" (a person who flies on commercial airlines with drugs in him/ her or in his/her possessions) in Lincolnshire. Rates of courier drug arrests—some of them called "swallowers" who are detected by X-ray machines in the airport—have soared in the UK. Between June 2002 and May 2003, for example, there was a jump in such arrests of 38 percent over the previous 12 months. By the time she returned to Jamaica, Georgette's children were in foster care. She would like to have her children back, but there is no room for them in the tiny shack she now lives in, located in a slum area called Bogue Hill on the outskirts of Montego Bay. Complicating Georgette's problems, because of overall high unemployment rates and stigmatization of ex-offenders, work is hard to come by. Notes Ash (2006), "Many ex-mules return to find that they have nowhere to live, their husbands or boyfriends are living with other women and their sons and daughters have become street children or have simply disappeared." Further, some are brutally beaten by the drug dealers for failing to deliver the cocaine and return with cash.

Aldrie Henry-Lee (2005), a Jamaican sociologist who has studied poverty on the island and the impact of imprisonment on Jamaican women, reports that the majority (86%) of the women she interviewed were incarcerated because of drug offenses. Like Georgette, most of the women (87.5%) indicated that their primary motivation for involvement in crime was economic deprivation. In addition to the long-term emotional and social impact of incarceration for the women, Henry-Lee found cause for concern about the effect on children's long-term development, including noting patterns of multigeneration involvement in crime.

The impact of drugs on families is not limited to involvement in drug trafficking but extends as well to the disruptive effects of drug use by family members. K. Boyce-Reid (1995), a social worker who has conducted ethnographic research on the impact of drug use on Jamaican families, reports on the damaging effects on family functioning and the health of other family members. Comments by female participants in Boyce-Reid's study included the following:

> My whole life is inside out; I feel I have no control over the situation. I am so caught up with [my son] that the other children feel

neglected and it is a strain for me to try to please everyone. I worry about him. I spend every waking moment wondering what is happening to my child. It is especially difficult when it rains and I don't know if he is in any form of shelter. I am only able to cope because of my religious belief.

I am forgetful, I cry a lot and I feel helpless. I have no control over him and he abuses me and the other children. I have migraine headaches and have to be under a doctor's care. I have no immediate family to help me but my employer has been very supportive.

With father out of the picture, the sole responsibility for caring for the children is mine. The problem affects my work, I cannot concentrate.

In this way, drinking and drug use among family members can contribute to household disruption and even economic breakdown, especially in households already on the very edge because of structural changes that make it ever more difficult to survive in a globalizing world. Drinking and drug use by family members threatens family assets and savings, which often are meager to begin with, making families ever more dependent on traditional household safety-net systems (e.g., extended family support). This can, in turn, lead to a downward spiral of increasing dependency, poorer nutrition and health within the family, and food shortages that decrease household viability. Ultimately, the ability of the family to function as an economic and social unit can be put at risk.

HEALTH CONSEQUENCES

The potential nutritional impacts of drug abuse noted above are among a considerable number of health and mental health problems associated with drug consumption in developing countries, most notably of which in recent decades has been HIV/AIDS.

AIDS and Tuberculosis

Acquired Immune Deficiency Syndrome (AIDS) has emerged as one of the most devastating diseases in human history. The global count of people living with HIV/AIDS infection reached 40 million by the end of 2004; millions more had already succumbed to the disease. Although HIV/AIDS is now found everywhere, it is not equally distributed among the populations and subpopulations of the world. One way of understanding the unequal spread of this disease is by examining the number of people living with HIV/AIDS along a geographic continuum. At one end of the continuum is sub-Saharan Africa, which remains the region hardest hit by the disease, with approximately

25.5 million people now living with HIV/AIDS infection and an adult (age 15–49) prevalence rate of 7.4 percent. Near the opposite end of the continuum falls North America, with about a million people living with HIV/AIDS and an adult prevalence rate of 0.6 percent, which is not significantly above that of Oceania, the region of the world with the lowest prevalence rate. Between these two epidemiological poles lie the island nations of the Caribbean, with under half a million cases and a prevalence rate of 2.3 percent. After sub-Saharan Africa, the Caribbean is now the second most intensely impacted region of the world (UNAIDS 2004). To get some sense of the impact of HIV/AIDS on national development, in Caribbean countries like Haiti and Trinidad it is believed that by the year 2010 life expectancy will be 9–10 years shorter than it would have been without the disease. In other words, while life expectancy is increasing in the U.S. and Europe despite the presence of HIV/AIDS, in many developing countries the disease is significantly shortening how long people live on average.

In 2005, there were over four million new HIV cases in developing nations, while almost three million people died of AIDS-related causes. Notably, from the standpoint of human resources for development, according to the UN Office on Drugs and Crime (2006), "One third of the people living with HIV/AIDS are between 15 and 24 years old." Now reported in 130 countries, injection drug use and the direct or indirect sharing of syringes and other injection equipment "[are] among the major forces driving the epidemic, contributing to around five per cent of HIV transmission" (UN Office on Drugs and Crime 2006). In Bangkok, Thailand, for example, the first cases of HIV among injection drug users were found among patients treated at the Thanyarak Hospital. After the first detection of these initial cases, HIV prevalence among injection drug users in Bangkok shot up from 1–2 percent in 1988 to 40 percent in 1989. Since then, HIV/AIDS surveillance has shown a steady level of prevalence of 30–50 percent in Bangkok and throughout the country (Razak et al. 2003, Vanichensi et al. 1991).

At the same time, the number of new tuberculosis cases in lesser developed countries has continued to grow by one percent a year. While HIV played an important role in the initial spread of tuberculosis (because of the damage HIV does to the immune system of the host) to new areas, increasingly it is spreading independent of HIV infection, a painful reflection of poverty and overcrowding. Almost two million people a year are now dying of tuberculosis in the developing world according to the UN.

The Syndemics of Drug Use

Increasingly the health problems of developing countries are not best characterized by terminology that points to the prevalence of individual diseases, such as terms like "epidemics" and "pandemics." Rather they are best described by terms like "syndemics" that point to social and biological interconnections in health as they are shaped and influenced by inequalities within and between societies. At its simplest level, the term syndemic refers to two or more epidemics (i.e., notable increases in the rate of specific diseases in a population), interacting synergistically with each other inside human bodies and contributing, as a result of their biological interaction, to an excess burden of disease in a population beyond what would otherwise be expected. The term syndemic refers not only to the temporal or locational co-occurrence of two or more diseases or health problems, but also to the health consequences of the biological interactions among copresent diseases, such between HIV and tuberculosis. HIV-positive individuals infected with TB, for example, are 100 times more likely to develop active disease than are those who are HIV-negative and TB-positive. Similarly, research has shown that individuals coinfected with hepatitis C (HCV) and HIV have higher HCV viral loads (i.e., levels of infectious agents in their bodies) than those infected with only HCV (Singer and Baer 2007).

Beyond the notion of disease clustering in a social location or population and the biological processes of interaction among diseases, the term syndemic also points to the critical importance of social conditions in disease interactions and consequences (Navarro 2001). As Farmer (1999:51–52) has emphasized, "the most well demonstrated cofactors [for HIV] are social inequalities, which structure not only the contours of the AIDS pandemic but also the nature of outcomes once an individual is sick with complications of HIV infection." Various syndemics have been described in the health literature on underdeveloped nations, including the hookworm, malaria and HIV/AIDS syndemic (Hotez 2003) and the Chagas disease, rheumatic heart disease and congestive heart failure syndemic (Cubillos-Garzon et al. 2004). Notably, drug use has been found to play a key role in various syndemics (Singer 2006b). Because they are characterized by a significant increase in the burden of disease, drug-based syndemics present a growing threat to development.

VIOLENCE

Violence and drugs are closely intertwined in the popular imagination. In communities in which drug use is embedded in community social life and limited by community expectations and sanctions, there is no natural connection between drug-induced altered states of consciousness and violence. In other contexts, however, deadly violence is a frequent and influential component of the drug domain. Even in these settings, violence is not random or meaningless; rather, it reflects the changing structure of relations in the global world. Notes E. Arias (2006:11): "The international debt crisis and structural adjustment have forced many states in the developing world to dramatically scale back services to their citizenry, and governments find themselves unable to adequately fund and train police to deal with the new challenges."

Illicit drug groups have stepped into the breach, engaging each other in violent confrontations over sources of income while, at the same time, offering weakened government officials the opportunity to "employ violence by proxy" to achieve their own ends (E. Arias 2006:12). Civic actors and government officials, in turn, can offer drug corporations protection from arrests and prosecution. In other words, the violence of drug-involved criminal groups may reflect broader political conflict rather than drug-specific ends. As a consequence, "drug violence" is magnified and extended to arenas of social life far beyond the furthering of drug-specific interests. The end result is enhanced social suffering among those directly and indirectly, intentionally and accidentally victimized by "drug violence."

Come to Jamaica

Without doubt, the world of illicit drug trafficking can be extremely violent; sometimes shockingly so. Exemplary of the intensive and enduring violence that can develop within the illicit drug trade, toward the end of 2005, Peter Philips, national security minister of Jamaica, announced that over 1,400 people had been killed during the year—in a country that has a total population of only 2.7 million. This was not a unique year as there had been over 1,400 homicide deaths on the island the previous year as well (as contrasted with 900 in the year 2000). Much of the increase in violence, Philips announced, was the result of turf wars over drugs and drug profits among rival gangs in the island nation well-known to the wider world because of its reggae music and tourist vacation resorts (*USA Today* 2005).

The regularity of drug-related violence in Jamaica is striking. Colin Grant (2002), a UK-born reporter for BBC News whose parents come from Jamaica, reported he was dismayed by the frequency of violence during a visit in 2002:

> Pouring over the papers on my first morning in the capital, Kingston, is an unsettling introduction to violence—Jamaican style. The headline from *The Star* screams: "Cop Executed!—Gangsters have killed an off-duty policeman, ambushed in his patrol car on his way home". Two mornings later—the same headline—different policeman—having a drink in his regular bar when gunmen burst in. Sprayed the bar with bullets, killing the officer and relieving him

of his gun. On the fourth day yet another policeman dead. . . .
Cocaine is again flooding the capital, and with it come gangs and
gunmen who have no fear of the law. Perversely, killing a policeman commands respect—a kind of kudos in certain aspects of gang-
ster life.

The shooting and targeted assassinations, Grant (2002) quickly real-
ized, are not one-sided. "[If] the gangsters are local celebrities then so
too are the policemen—with nicknames like 'Cowboy' and 'Fast Draw.'
In such a climate it is unsurprising that there have been numerous
accusations of unlawful killings by police officers."

The end result is the production of a deadly drug-related culture
of violence. One victim of this milieu was Grant's colleague Hugh
Crosskill, a former BBC journalist who was shot to death in Jamaica
in 2002 (BBC News 2002). One of the Caribbean's best-known and
prominent reporters who had been a role model for many journalists
in the Caribbean, Crosskill had fallen on hard times and was battling
a drug addiction at the time of his death, which resulted from an argument with a security guard in the Jamaican capital of Kingston. San-
dra Ann, a Jamaican friend of Crosskill, told BBC News: "The security
guard may well have held the 'smoking gun,' but, without a doubt, it
was the drug dealers who killed Hugh."

The Most Violent Place on Earth

The same pattern of drug-related violence emerged in Haiti after
2004. It is well-known that Haiti, a nation just somewhat larger than
the state of Maryland, is extremely poor and has a notably weak and
unstable government; it has been dubbed a failed state in the current
parlance of the international development sector. When Human
Rights Watch (2006) observers visited Haiti in 2005, they found that
the police were understaffed and poorly trained to investigate crimes
and the judicial system was barely functional. Conditions in the country are grim. Seven out of ten Haitians live on less than $2 a day;
inhabitants of the island nation have life expectancies of only 52
years; 75 percent of the population live under the poverty level; child
mortality rates are 128 per thousand; illiteracy among teenagers and
young adults is over 65 percent (Revol 2006). Among the poorest parts
of urban Haiti is a squalid seaside shantytown area on the northern
edge of the capital of Port-au-Prince known as Cité Soleil (Sun City),
which in 2004 the UN labeled "the most dangerous place on earth"
(Muralidhar 2007). Approximately five square kilometers in size, this
highly marginalized community of overcrowded and suffocatingly hot
makeshift tin structures, muddy and garbage-strewn pathways, mal-
nutrition and overt starvation, and disease, misery and death, has
come to epitomize the face of social suffering in Haiti (Maternowska
2006). Its (roughly) 200,000–300,000 residents, many of them

migrants from rural parts of the country, fell fully under the control of several armed, drug-involved gangs in 2004.

Fourteen-year-old Cité Soleil resident, herself a shooting victim, Edna St. Plus told *Miami Herald* reporter Joe Mozingo (2005), "Chimres [literally ghosts, the creole term used for drug gangs] are killing people in the streets. . . . They try to stop drivers and if the drivers don't stop, they just shoot them. That hurts, to see someone killed for a car." Observed Mozingo (2005):

> Young men openly roam the streets with assault weapons and World War II-era rifles. Even younger boys—some not even teenagers yet—patrol the main roads. They often look stoned and furiously question visitors at gunpoint.

These youthful gang soldiers do not wander aimlessly but rather within defined borders that segment parts of the community from each other based on the territories controlled by rival gangs. Adds anthropologist Catherine Maternowska, who conducted research in Cité Soleil at various points between the mid-1980s and 2005, "the buying and selling of drugs has consumed the community" (2006:58).

Drugs are not new to Haiti. Colombia-based illicit drug corporations have long taken advantage of the political instability of Haiti to use it as central transit point for cocaine shipments to the U.S. The island of Hispaniola, which Haiti shares with the Dominican Republic, is only about 400 miles from Colombia's northernmost point, making it readily accessible by a twin-engine airplane loaded with 500 or more kilos of powder cocaine. Commercial ships also are used to bring cocaine to the island, as these have large cargo and passenger sections in which smugglers can construct hidden compartments for illicit drugs. Haitian drug trafficking groups make use of narrow wooden-hulled boats, called *yolas,* many of them painted the color of sea water, to move cocaine to transshipment sites, as these traditional boats lie low in the water, allowing smugglers to avoid detection by radar. Cité Soleil, with its large, poorly maintained waterfront, provides an entry and exit point for drug shipments. Cocaine moves out of the country aboard coastal freighters destined for the U.S. or Europe, although other methods, including individual drug mules, are also used.

In 2000, the U.S. State Department (Marshall 2001) reported that drug traffickers sent about 15 percent of the cocaine that reached the U.S. the previous year (approximately 75 tons) through Haiti, up about 25 percent from the previous year. Three years earlier, the head of the Drug Enforcement Administration (DEA), J. Milford (1997), testifying before the U.S. Congress on the drug trade in Haiti, remarked:

> As in most locations where the cocaine trade flourishes, competition for control of the local market has resulted in an escalation of drug-related crime. Tragically, as we have seen in Colombia, Mex-

ico and the United States, violence and corruption are attendant to the drug trade. Drug corruption is rampant, even in the police and judicial system.

Frank Figueroa, who served in the Miami Customs Service during this period, attributed Haiti's transshipment role in the Colombia-to-U.S. cocaine flow to the weak nature of the Haitian government:

> I think the instability right now in that country is lending itself as an area of vulnerability. . . . The Colombian cartels have realised that, and traffickers are always looking for that weak link in the chain. It just so happens that Haiti is that weak link. (quoted in Greste 2000)

By "weak link" the DEA refers to the fact that

> the country lacks the resources, political will and law enforcement infrastructure needed to significantly impact drug trafficking operations and organizations. Intelligence indicates that corruption is deeply rooted throughout the Haitian government, further hindering law enforcement efforts. (Marshall 2001)

The reasons for Haiti's role as a "weak link" were specified by Jean-Bertrand Aristide in a speech before the General Assembly of the United Nations in the early 1990 just prior to his return to the presidency of the country. He noted that the Haitian military earned as much as $200 million a year for facilitating the flow of drugs through the country. With the subsequent second overthrow of the Aristide government, however, the impact of drugs on places like Cité Soleil took on devastating proportions. As Maternowska (2006:12) reports, within Cité Soleil "shootings, burning barricades or buildings, brutal beatings of innocent people . . . were commonplace." So too was death. Maternowska observed 22 corpses dumped on the filthy roads of Cité Soleil (their faces severed to hinder identification) during a single two-month period of research.

Violence: It's Only Business

Like all corporate heads, the CEOs of illicit drug corporations face a variety of challenges on the road to success. Functioning in a subterranean world of illegality, the day-to-day operating procedures in the illicit drug trade comprise a mix of standard business practices (e.g., developing workforce supervision and quality-control procedures, implementing computer-based accounting systems, and purchasing transport vehicles on the open market) and a set of additional strategies that in and of themselves (aside from the illicit product in question) are illegal, such as the use of threats, intimidation, and physical violence. Indeed, part of the public reputation of illicit drug corporations is that they are cut-throat and prepared to use extreme measures, as seen, for example, in the illicit cocaine corporations of Medellín, Colombia.

The Drug Enforcement Administration uses the term "source country" to refer to the places where illicit drugs originate. Colombia has consistently shown up on DEA source country lists as a primary supplier of marijuana, cocaine, and heroin. While violence was always part of the illicit cocaine scene in Colombia, during the late 1980s and early 1990s the use of extreme violence to achieve the aims of the illicit drug corporations of Medellín reached a pinnacle.

During this period, illicit drug manufacturers were under increasing pressure from the Colombian government and their U.S. supporters as a result of the War on Drugs. To undermine the legal attack launched against them, the cocaine corporations sought to intimidate judges and other sectors of the criminal justice system and society at large. All told, almost 500 police and 40 judges were killed, leading to a strike by judicial employees protesting the failure of the government to protect them. The illegal drug corporations were also implicated in the murder of a minister of justice, a leader of the Patriotic Union political party, the governor of the state of Antioquia, the attorney general of Colombia, and the leading liberal party candidate for the 1990 presidential election. Additionally, numerous car bombs were detonated resulting in the deaths of over 500 people, mostly civilians. In Bogotá, the façade of the Department of Administrative Security headquarters was blown off, killing 100 people. Bombs were placed in banks, hotels, the offices of political parties, and in commercial centers. In one case, over a hundred passengers were killed by an explosive loaded aboard an Avianca flight from Bogotá to Cali. In the end, this campaign of violence achieved some of its intended goals, such as defeat of the Colombia–U.S. extradition treaty, which would have permitted the extradition of illicit drug traffickers from Colombia to the U.S. for prosecution.

The most vicious and intense violence exhibited by illegal drug corporations is reserved usually for competitors, especially during periods when a drug market has been disrupted in some fashion. A typical case occurred along the Mexican border in 2003 when a highly lucrative drug trade was thrown into disarray after Mexican police arrested the leader of the so-called "Gulf Cartel." Seeing an opening, a rival illicit drug corporation, the "Sinaloa Cartel" sent a representative to take over the cocaine and methamphetamine drug smuggling routes in the vicinity of Nuevo Laredo, Mexico. In defense of their "turf" the Gulf Cartel called on Los Zetas, a group of Mexican special forces officers who had deserted the military to serve as muscle in the illegal drug trade. An all-out drug war erupted across Mexico that left about 1,000 people dead (Thomas 2005).

These examples suggest some of potential for violence in the illegal drug trade. Because it can endure for long periods, such violence not only inflicts injuries and death, it also wears away at the fabric of society and diverts resources that are sorely needed for national development.

ADDRESSING BOTH SIDES OF THE DRUG THREAT

As Mesquita, based on the experience of Brazil, has stressed, "The developing world is extremely affected by the health and social impacts of the illicit drug market" (2006:66). While agreeing with Mesquita, it is an argument of this book that the legal drug market, as well as illicit activities among legal drug corporations, also contribute to significant health and social problems that undermine development efforts. Stressing that both arms of the dual drug market, legal and illegal, are a threat to development is critical because of the tendency of official pronouncements to equate drug trafficking and terrorism, as indicated by the increasingly frequent use of the phrase "narcoterrorism" in the development discourse. In fact, it can reasonably be argued that legal drugs like tobacco and alcohol have at least as great if not a considerably greater impact on development internationally than do illegal drugs and that development policy would benefit from a focus on what might be called "nico-ethanol-terrorism" (e.g., corporate promotion of nicotine and ethanol addiction and disease).

Both legal and illegal drugs contribute to the maintenance of social inequality internationally because they perpetuate and exacerbate underdevelopment. Avoiding what has been called "drug compartmentalization" (i.e., treating legal and illegal substances as if they were innately different entities) and effectively addressing *both* sides of the drug issue is a critical step for developing nations and for the wider array of organizations and institutions that promote social and economic development around the world. This point underlines the importance of examining "drug control policy," a task taken up in chapter 4.

Chapter Four

International Drug Control Policy and National Development

Drugs seized in imported toys at Port of Durban, South Africa.

COMMON GOALS OR CROSS-PURPOSES?

Policy analysts differentiate two types of policy: the first, reactive policy, is present-oriented and emerges as policy makers implement immediate measures in response to a threatening crisis, such as a health emergency; the second, proactive policy, is more future-oriented and is guided by a longer-term vision of an aspired future, such as achievement of a broader foundation for democracy or higher standard of living. While national and international drug control policies tend to be reactive in nature, development policy to a greater degree is guided by a proactive orientation. Herein resides one point of potential tension between drug control and sustainable development policies. Other contradictions have been identified as well. Most notably, drug control policy with its narrow focus on very specific goals (e.g., eradicating drug crops, interdiction of smuggled drug shipments, arrest of so-called "drug king-pins" or users) and its tendency to be linked with broader political economic issues, can run roughshod over targeted objectives of development, such as expanding civil liberties and social justice.

Without doubt, as the prior chapters emphasize, both legal and illegal drugs, and their respective means of distribution and consumption, have significant if varied impacts on the health and well-being of people in developing nations. Yet, as the contributors to the book *Drugs and Justice* (Battin et al. 2008) stress, the drug policies that have been developed ostensibly to minimize the damage caused by drugs commonly are burdened by significant contradictions and secondary agendas. For example, as physician and lawyer Peter Cohen (2008:vii–viii) of the Georgetown University Law Center asks: "Why do we allow the sale of alcohol and tobacco, both responsible for greater rates of mortality and morbidity than 'illegal drugs'? No doubt, among the many factors responsible for the disjunction between scientific fact and public policy are the overwhelming influences of money and lobbying" by drug corporations.

Thus, it is necessary to go beyond assessing the negative effects of drugs and ask the question: What are the health and social impacts of drug control policy? In addressing this query, this chapter examines the relationship of drug control efforts to national development objectives. Additionally, the chapter seeks to answer several related questions, namely: In that legal and illegal drugs present significant challenges for underdeveloped nations, by controlling the influx or consumption of drugs do control campaigns accelerate development? As a result, might controlling drugs be understood as a necessary and indispensable step in national development? Indeed, in the developing world should drug control programs, like the War on Drugs, be considered development programs?

Answering these questions is imperative because the contemporary discourse on global patterns of drug use often depicts the contemporary War on Drugs as a complement to if not an actual component of national progress in underdeveloped countries. The United Nations Office on Drugs and Crime (UNODC) (1994:1), for example, in noting that "there has been growing attention on substance abuse as a detriment to development" asserts that there are common solutions to the pressing problems in developing countries to be found in uniting the fields of development and drug control. Unification is possible, UNODC maintains, because the tools and goals of drug control and national development ultimately are quite similar:

> As a better understanding of the linkage between drug abuse and underdevelopment spreads throughout the world, there will inevitably be greater recognition of the fact that drug control's ultimate aim is to help people. Effective drug control means steering children away from a life of crime. It means assisting individuals to reintegrate into civil society. It means making sure that Governments do not benefit from illegal earnings. It means helping peasants to make a better life without having to fear the law. It means assisting countries to recover from the ravages of war. It means preventing people from getting AIDS. (United Nations Office on Drugs and Crime 1994:15)

Concrete examples of unities in drug control and development noted by various UN bodies and reports include: (1) joint educational efforts for youth in which development programs concentrate on improving schools and expanding educational resources while drug control programs infuse school curricula with drug use prevention information and help reintegrate recovering drug abusing youth into the school system; (2) rural development initiatives, including the provision of seeds, equipment, training, and marketing assistance that offer small farmers, most of whom are quite poor (a group thought to number five million worldwide) realistic alternatives to the cultivation of plants that contain psychotropic substances; (3) postwar reconstruction involving a coordinated division of labor, with development programs focusing on issues like the humanitarian reintegration of refugees and drug control schemes focusing on blocking attempts to use returning refugees to smuggle-in illicit drugs; and (4) community health promotion activities that benefit from the arrest of individuals engaged in drug-related risk behavior.

To provide context for assessing the accuracy of these assertions, as well to provide case materials to use in answering the questions listed above, we begin with brief glimpses at contemporary drug control efforts in four different developing nations: Guyana, Tajikistan, China, and Afghanistan.

DRUG CONTROL EFFORTS IN FOUR DEVELOPING NATIONS

Nondrug Control in Guyana

As described in chapter 1, the South American country of Guyana has been significantly impacted by the international drug trade since it became an important transshipment hub for cocaine destined primarily for North America but also for the countries of Europe and the island nations of the Caribbean. Despite expressed commitment to controlling the flow of drugs through the country, as seen in the development of a National Drug Strategy Master Plan for 2005–2009, the government of Guyana has been unable to control the flow of drugs because it lacks the internal management and coordination, resources (e.g. patrol sea- and aircraft), and a trained workforce needed to stop drug traffickers from moving drug shipments through the country, almost at will. Guyana's remote and largely unregulated borders and coastline, and its extensive, lightly populated, and minimally policed rain forests provide excellent conditions for drug smuggling. Corrupt local, regional, and national officials and business operators—individuals tempted by the payoffs of the wealthy drug corporations, as well as intimidated by their threats—facilitate the ready movement of drugs into and out of the country.

Drug shipments are driven into Guyana across minimally patrolled borders from neighboring Brazil, Suriname, and Venezuela. They are moved through the country to the capital, Georgetown, by small boats and freighters along Guyana's many navigable rivers. In the capital, they are packed onto "go-fast" boats that transport them to cargo ships waiting offshore for their illicit freight, or they are smuggled aboard commercial air carriers. Other creative means of transport also are used. In July of 2006, for example, Spanish police discovered a drug-smuggling corporation that used expensive yachts rented out for wealthy family holidays to move its product. Spanish officials reported that cocaine was loaded onto the yachts in Guyana, Venezuela, and Suriname and concealed below the decks while paying passengers enjoyed their ocean cruises unaware of the hidden cargo. Drug traffickers also have concealed drug shipments in every commodity that Guyana exports to other countries. Whatever their method of transport or circuitous route of movement, ultimately the drugs either are seized by law enforcement authorities, are lost or abandoned because of weather or fear of detection, are stolen, or arrive at their destination on the streets of New York or Madrid or other world cities.

Drug interdiction in Guyana is limited at best. In 2006, for example, Guyanese law enforcement officers seized less than 60 kgs of cocaine. Not one of the publicly reported drug seizures were greater than 10 kgs. This is believed to be an insignificant portion of the cocaine that actually was moved through Guyana that year. During 2006, Guyanese law enforcement officials arrested several dozen drug couriers at Guyana's international airport. They were found to have targeted virtually every northbound air route out of the country. But the individuals who were arrested were all low-level "drug mules" carrying small quantities of marijuana, crack cocaine, or powder cocaine to distant customers. There were no arrests of major drug traffickers in Guyana or any significant government threat to the operations of their drug corporations. During the year, however, Shaheed "Roger" Khan, a Guyanese businessman, and three ex-policemen were arrested on drug smuggling charges in neighboring Suriname (Stra-broek News 2006). Over 200 kgs of cocaine were seized during the police operation. Prior to his arrest, a U.S. grand jury in Brooklyn, New York, had indicted Khan for violating Sections 952 and 963, Title 21, of the United States Code (smuggling illicit drugs). Khan claimed that as an Indo-Guyanese citizen he was the victim of corrupt Afro-Guyanese government officials. Following his arrest, under the guise of being deported to Guyana, Khan was sent to Trinidad and Tobago, where he was turned over to U.S. authorities and extradited to New York pending a trial on 18 drug charges. Political activists in Guyana have protested the heavy U.S. hand in seizing and deporting a Guyanese citizen, a charge that has simply been ignored by U.S. officials.

Guyana, in short, like many developing nations with a weak national government and an impoverished population, is unable to control its drug problem. In no small part, lack of internal control of drugs reflects Guyana's weak position in the global economy, as detailed in chapter 1. Elsewhere, however, the governments of a few poor developing nations, such as Tajikistan, have claimed—amid controversy as seen below—that they have in fact established quite effective drug control initiatives.

Claiming Success in Tajikistan

In light of the significance of its drug problem, as described in chapter 1, in 2002 the United Nations' Drug Control Program provided Tajikistan with funding for a Drug Control Agency that now styles itself as a model for the wider region. Funds also have been contributed by the U.S. for equipment, training, and the development of mobile units to interdict Afghan drug consignments moving through Tajikistan. The Tajikistan government has publicly complained that promises of similar assistance from Russia have not been fulfilled.

The Drug Control Agency with its staff of 350 workers is responsible for coordinating all government efforts involving drug interdiction, drug abuse prevention, and drug treatment. Drug control agents, whose behavior is closely monitored, are paid $170 a month, or about $160 per month more than the average worker in the country. The goal is to pay agents enough to limit the temptation to accept one of the many bribes they are likely to be offered. In 2001, agents seized over four tons of heroin, compared to just ten kilograms seized during a similar period ten years previously (Constable 2002). Two years later, the agency boasted seizures of approximately ten tons of opium and heroin and was praised by Antonio Maria Costa, executive director of the UNODC, who commented:

> The establishment of the Drug Control Agency in Tajikistan is a milestone in the history of drug control in the region. Over the past five years, Tajikistan has become one of the leading countries in the world in opiates interceptions. (United Nations Information Service 2004)

Nonetheless, in January of 2004, a very high-ranking officer of the Drug Control Agency that was posted in Tajikistan's Zaravshan Valley was arrested with 30 kilograms of heroin, and an additional six kilograms of opium were found at his home. Similarly, in August 2004, the commander of the Presidential Guard and director of the Drug Control Agency, Gaffor Mirzoevy, was arrested for various crimes, and reportedly was involved in organizing drug smuggling into Russia. According to Kairat Osmonaliev (2006:3), head of the law program at the Center of Post-Graduate Programs at Kyrgyz National University, there are various reports that "the Drug Control Agency itself is a body that has been penetrated by corruption."

In short, it is far from clear that Tajikistan, even with considerable outside aid and large drug seizures, has, in fact, succeeded in controlling the flow of illegal drugs or its corrupting influences.

Drug Control and Nation Building in China

A third example of the nature of national drug control efforts is presented by the People's Republic of China, which has a history of mounting intense waves of drug control crusades. On June 26, 1992, for example, an antiheroin rally was held in the municipal stadium in Kunming, the capital city of Yunnan Province, located on the far southwestern corner of the country. Four thousand people attended. As part of the activities of the public gathering, several arrested drug traffickers were put on trial, found guilty, and sentenced to death, where upon they were executed by a firing squad. In the aftermath of the execution, the provincial governor gave a speech in which he affirmed the government's unwavering commitment to fighting the rampant spread of illicit drug use. Next on the agenda was the public burning of 4,000 kilograms of heroin and opium in a series of electrical pots set up in one corner of the busy stadium. On the same day, near Guangzhou, the capital of Guangdong Province, on the southern edge of China, 160 kilograms of drugs were burned while 18 drug offenders were executed in the city of Guangzhou. June 26, International Anti-Narcotics Day (and the anniversary of the First Opium War in China), has become the focus of annual antidrug activities in China. The burning of drugs is the central ritual of these events and was depicted as a grand spectacle in the Chinese film *The Opium War* that was produced in 1997 to commemorate the reabsorption of Hong Kong (which was taken by the British during the First Opium War). Indeed, Yongming (1997) has argued that antidrug crusades have filled an important, if complex (and both locally and temporally varying), state-building function in twentieth-century China, serving as rites of intensification of Chinese nationalism. As he argues:

> Nationalism plays a major role in the making of a mainstream, anti-drug discourse in modern China, in the interpretations of the history of the Opium Wars, in the mobilizing of the social elite and general public in the cause of drug suppression, and even in the linking of drugs to the survival of the Chinese nation in the face of foreign aggression and threat. (Yongming 1997:170)

In short, in China, the modernist project of state building invokes, as a form of cultural intimacy (Herzfeld 2005), the shared painful and embarrassing memory of a British imperialism and the role of drugs in that historic if now culturally useful relationship. As this example suggests, drug control programs can and often are many things at once, including being social mechanisms for achieving goals that have little to do with containing illicit substances.

The Fall and Rise of Opium in Afghanistan

A final case of drug control efforts in a developing nation is found in the Taliban antidrug program in Afghanistan. In 2000, the Taliban, the Sunni Muslim and ethnic Pashtun movement that ruled most of Afghanistan from 1996 until pushed out by a U.S.–led invasion in 2001, implemented a ban on opium production that achieved a "99% reduction in the land area under opium poppy cultivation in Taliban-controlled areas" (Farrell and Thorne 2005:81) and proved to be one of the most effective drug control efforts in an underdeveloped country in modern times. As Jelsma details:

> It was a rare historical moment that allowed almost absolute com-pliance in the south of the country, with hardly any direct enforce-ment or punishment required. From the eastern regions, where Taliban control was far from absolute, several cases of disobedience were reported, largely resolved by means of negotiations and pay-offs to local warlords. By harvest time in spring 2001, the effective-ness of the ban was already confirmed beyond any doubt, and astonished the international community at the time. (2005:1)

These efforts were launched following Taliban discussions with the director of the UN Office of Drug Control, Pino Arlacchi, that included a UN offer of $250 million as compensation for lost revenues and the possibility of international recognition of the Taliban regime. Instead, following the announcement of the ban by Mullah Mohammed Omar, head of the Taliban government, Arlacchi, to the

Two Afghan men caught smuggling heroin. (Photo by Stefano Zardini)

great surprise of his own in-country staff, moved to shut down all UN drug control initiatives in Afghanistan. The Taliban responded with dismay and anger. Director of the Taliban High Commission for Drug Control, Abdel Hamid Akhundzada, declared, "We have done what needed to be done, putting our people and our farmers through immense difficulties. We expected to be rewarded for our actions, but instead were punished with additional sanctions" (quoted in Transnational Institute 2001).

One consequence of the short-lived successful Taliban drug control program (which, as noted in chapter 2, was dissolved with the U.S.-led invasion, resulting in a momentous expansion of Afghan poppy cultivation) was a notable drop in the purity of heroin available on world illicit drug markets. The Forensic Science Service in the UK, for example, which monitors heroin samples, found a notable decline in purity from 55 percent during the first quarter of 2001 down to 34 percent in the second quarter of following year (United Nations Office for Drug Control 2003). There is speculation that rises in drug-related deaths following the ban in countries supplied by Afghanistan may have been a result of drug use dynamics involving the use of dangerous substances to "cut" street heroin (and thereby keep up profits when actual drug supplies were down); reverting to the use of contaminated low-quality heroin sources (such as "kompot" or poppy straw); increased consumption through intravenous injection (to derive the most impactful "high" available with adulterated products); and street diversion of synthetic analgesics (e.g., Spasmo Proxyvon, a nonsoluble opioid that when injected clings to the walls of the veins causing abscesses that can lead to amputation). In other words, the "success" of the Taliban drug control program came at tremendous cost for drug users. Hit with a heroin shortage, heroin sellers and users did not end their involvement with drugs, rather they adapted by switching to other (potentially more dangerous) drugs, drug combinations, and means of consumption (Jelsma 2005).

The four contrasting examples presented above reveal the complexities and challenges of understanding the nature and impact of national and international drug control initiatives, as further revealed by reviewing drug control in historic perspective.

DRUG CONTROL: A HISTORIC PERSPECTIVE

Government initiatives designed to control drug manufacture, trafficking, and use are not new (Andreas and Nadelmann 2006). It has been argued that the earliest effort to prohibit the use of psychotropic substances dates to the Qur'anic ban on alcohol and perhaps other intoxicants dating to the seventh century. Early efforts to rigorously enforce this ban include eleventh- and twelfth-century Egyptian campaigns to abolish Sufi use of hashish—used by them to facilitate direct mystical experience of the divine—by burning cultivated fields of marijuana and publicly torturing Sufi hashish users (Abel 1982). In that most followers of the Sufi tradition were of lower-class origin, and their behavior was seen as a class challenge to the established social order, the attempt to control Sufi drug use very likely had its origin in the political motives of dominant social groups in Egyptian society to restrict a potential threat from below. Similarly, during the fourteenth century, the emir of Joneiama in Eygpt, Soudon Sheikhouni, outlawed marijuana use among the poor, ordered the eradication of marijuana fields, had offenders' teeth pulled out during public ceremonies, and then put the victims in prison (Hanrahan 2002). As Robinson (1996) points out, however, the emir's punishments had no lasting effect, as marijuana use persisted in Egypt. Nonetheless, social control, sometimes violently enforced, of subordinate or other marginalized but potentially rebellious groups has been a very common theme in drug control efforts ever since.

The Inquisition adopted equally brutal if similarly unsuccessful methods to eradicate marijuana use among Arabs in Spain following a decree issued by Pope Innocent VIII in 1484 that asserted the drug was an unholy sacrament of the Satanic mass. The Spanish also carried the antidrug campaign of the Inquisition to the New World, and during the seventeenth century attempted to eradicate peyote use among indigenous peoples of Mexico (Lang 2004) (as well as coca-leaf chewing among the Indians of South America). Ironically, although peyote, a cactus that produces psychotropic alkaloids like mescaline, was consumed in religious rituals (as well as medicinally), the Inquisition decried this practice as a diabolical crime against God. As a result, beginning in 1620, sixty years after the sacramental use of the drug in Mexico was first described by the Franciscan Friar Bernardino de Sahagún, Indians caught using peyote were tortured and burned at the stake by Spanish priests. Despite their severity, these and subsequent tactics used by both Mexican and later American officials failed to stamp out indigenous use of peyote, and, over time, the practice spread to other native peoples similarly suffering under the yoke of external domination on both sides of the Mexico–U.S. border.

Over time, the drug-control agenda of the entire world has been set by decisions made by government bodies north of the U.S.–Mexico border, making drug control in the U.S. a critical feature of the international history of drug containment.

The Rise of Drug Control Efforts in the United States

During the colonial era in the U.S., drugs like the opiates, marijuana, cocaine, and alcohol were everyday items of legal trade and consumption. While their potency and potential harmful effects were well-known, the right of people to sell, possess, and use them was not generally called into question. The origin of legal restriction on the sale and use of drugs in the U.S. dates to the final decades of the nineteenth century (Erlen and Spillane 2004) as the U.S. emerged as a major player on the international political and economic scene, was the recipient of an extensive migration of people from many lands, and became, in the process, an ethnically far more complex country. The targets of the first American drug control laws were so-called opium dens that usually were found in the segregated Chinese sections of western cities, although their customers included both Chinese and non-Chinese people alike.

The very first drug law in the nation was passed in San Francisco in 1875, home to a large immigrant Chinese population. Publicly, during this period, smoking opium began to be labeled deviant and debilitating, but the real driving force behind passage of the law was anti-Asian hysteria. Hence, the primary concern was not drug use *per se*, or potentially harmful effects, but rather *who* was using drugs and, more so, who was profiting from drug sales. Further, opium smoking was outlawed because Bay-area officials feared that Chinese men were using it to lure innocent white women into drug dens and into a life of prostitution and sexual debauchery. The racist sentiments driving passage of the law are revealed by a court case from the period involving the arrest and conviction of a Chinese man for opium sales. A legal review of the case soon after it occurred concluded, "Smoking opium is not our vice, and therefore, it may be that this legislation proceeds more from a desire to vex and annoy the 'Heathen Chinese' in this respect, than to protect the people from the evil habit" (quoted in Bonnie and Whitebread 1970:997).

From this point on, U.S. societal reactions to drug use and attitudes about particular ethnic groups were closely entwined and played a significant role in driving internal drug control efforts. As the country moved toward the twentieth century, various kinds of drug use (but not others) came to be culturally constructed as public problems in America society. In the case of Chinese opium smoking, a major event that promoted the desire for social control was the depression that began in the 1860s. This economic downturn contributed to a social redefinition of the Chinese as an unwanted and surplus labor force. Recruited to build the national railroad system linking the eastern and western halves of the United States and to toil underground in the country's mines—activities that were integral to American national development—the Chinese subsequently were scapegoated as the cause of working-class suffering as the economy collapsed and people were pushed into unemployment. These developments led to the Chinese Exclusion Act of 1882, which outlawed further immigration from China. It was at this point that drug use practices that were defined as Chinese in origin emerged as behaviors in need of strict social control, while other drug use was ignored by lawmakers.

Late nineteenth-century attitudes and policies about cocaine similarly were in no small measure shaped by racism (which, in turn, was used to promote cocaine control). In particular, southern whites came to believe that if African Americans had access to cocaine they "might become oblivious of their prescribed bounds and attack white society" (Musto 1987:6). Claiming that "many of the horrible crimes committed in the Southern States by colored people can be traced directly to the cocaine habit" (quoted in Goode 1984:186), Colonel J. W. Watson of Georgia gave voice to this hate-fueled panic in a 1903 article in the *New York Tribune*. Similarly, the *New York Times* during this troubled era published an expose entitled "Negro Cocaine Fiends Are a New Southern Menace" that described Blacks as "running amuck in a cocaine frenzy" (quoted in Goode 1984:186). Popular literature at the time commonly played on white insecurities. Cocaine was portrayed as a drug that heightened the desire of Black men to rape white women. Erased from view by such assertions—and perhaps consciously so— was the fact that African Americans were the victims, not the perpetrators, of most of the racially motivated hate and sex crimes committed in the South during this period. Nonetheless, a deep-seated "fear of . . . cocainized Blacks" developed coincident "with the peak of lynchings, legal segregation, and [the passage of] voting laws . . . designed to remove political and social power from [Blacks]" (Musto 1987:7). One of the more peculiar beliefs about cocaine that developed was the notion that the drug made African Americans impervious to "mere .32 caliber bullets, [a belief that] is said to have caused southern police departments to switch to .38 caliber revolvers" (Musto 1987:7). To insure that cocaine in any form did not reach African Americans, it was dropped as an ingredient in Coca-Cola in 1903 and replaced by another stimulant, caffeine.

Efforts to convince the public that cocaine was particularly dangerous in the hands of African Americans were motivated in part by an attempt to persuade Congressmen from southern states to support the Harrison Narcotics Act (Drug Policy Alliance 2007a). This law (see below), which grew out of the International Opium Convention of 1912 and was pushed by Secretary of State William Jennings Bryan on the grounds that it fulfilled U.S. obligations stemming from the convention, began the process of federal drug criminalization in the U.S. The Harrison Narcotics Act did not actually outlaw drug use but it did empower the federal government to control and tax it and paved the way for subsequent bans.

The process of marijuana criminalization parallels the pattern seen with opium and cocaine. It began at the state level, in Utah in 1914, followed by New Mexico and Texas, at a point in time when most people in the U.S. were not aware of the drug. The ethnic group of concern in the push to criminalize marijuana was Mexican Americans. The assertion that "All Mexicans are crazy, and this stuff is what makes them crazy" was voiced on the floor of the Texas legislature in support of passage of marijuana control legislation (Drug Policy Alliance 2007b). In states that had large Mexican immigrant and Mexican American populations, the fear of marijuana grew intense (Musto 1987). In the public imagination in the Southwest and parts of the South, the picture of the marijuana-smoking, violent Mexican gained a prominent place in the imagination of non-Latino white citizens. By the time of the Great Depression, these prejudicial sentiments reached fever pitch, fueling the twin drives to control both marijuana use and Mexican immigration through the enactment of various (ultimately failed) policy initiatives.

International Drug Control in the Modern Era

Beyond the U.S., the rise of the unifying processes of globalism moved drug control initiatives to a new plane and led to the development of modern international drug control regimes (Bayer and Ghodse 1999). The term "regime" refers to the multination development of a set of rules and decision-making processes that require countries to agree to defer their sovereignty to an international body around a particular issue. Drug control regimes constitute one of the oldest forms of multilateral cooperation, predating the emergence of both the League of Nations and its successor, the United Nations. The International Opium Commission, composed of 13 countries, for example, was convened in Shanghai, China, in 1909 and gave rise to the first international drug control agreement: the Hague Opium Convention of 1912. This treaty, which established, in basic form, the present narcotics control regime, included restrictions on the import and export of poppy's various psychoactive derivatives.

In subsequent years, with the emergence of the League of Nations 1913, a long list of such international agreements designed to expand and tighten-up drug control efforts followed, including: the second International Opium Convention in 1925, which required opium-producing nations to sell opium only through government-run monopolies and to end the international opium trade completely by 1940 (as well, it established the first restrictions on marijuana distribution); the Convention for Limiting the Manufacture and Regulating the Distribution of Narcotic Drugs in 1931, which implemented a drug schedule for two kinds of drugs, one seen as more harmful and in need of greater control than the other; and the Convention for the Suppression of the Illicit Traffic in Dangerous Drugs in 1936, which was a failed attempt to get countries to criminalize all aspects of heroin, cocaine, and marijuana cultivation, manufacture, and distribution. Not surprisingly, during the Second World War, there were no international drug control meetings (as drug flows slowed significantly during this period, as reflected, for example, in notable drops in drug arrests and hospitalizations).

With the birth of the United Nations after the war, and the development of the second wave of globalism, the pattern of international conventions against drug trafficking and use began again and expanded in scope and level of enforcement. In 1946, to replace the League of Nation's Advisory Committee, the UN established the Commission on Narcotic Drugs as its policy-making body on international drug issues. Additionally, the commission was charged with monitoring the world drug situation and developing strategies for new international drug control efforts. Two years later, the UN implemented a policy to bring newly created synthetic drugs under international control. Increased regulation of poppy products came in 1953 with the Opium Protocol. In 1961, the Single Convention on Narcotic Drugs was established, and 116 narcotic drugs were identified as meriting international control. The convention also led to the creation of the generally quite conservative International Narcotics Control Board to monitor the extent to which member countries implement UN drug control agreements. Unlike many UN drug initiatives, the board has been sharply criticized for it tendency to go beyond its original mission to condemn efforts like harm reduction (e.g., Australia's safe heroin injection centers or Canada's approval of medicinal use of marijuana) that promote the health of drug users without taking a punitive approach to drug use. Ten years later, the Convention on Psychotropic Substances was implemented, which extended international control to include increasingly popular synthetically produced hallucinogens like LSD and mescaline, as well as pharmaceutical stimulants and barbiturates diverted for street use (while it also strengthened provisions against drug-related money laundering). In 1988, the United Nations Convention Against Illicit Traffic in Narcotic Drugs and Psychotropic Substances addressed the problem of international trade in "precursor" chemicals used in drug production. This century-long pattern of initiating new conventions every 5–15 or so years reflects the changing world of drug use (i.e., drug use dynamics) as well as the changing nature of relations among nations.

In 1997, the Office on Drugs and Crime (UNODC) was set up, and five years later Antonio Maria Costa, a University of California–trained economist, was appointed as its executive director. Among other tasks, the UNODC, an entity known for its energetic drive to play a lead role in international drug issues, releases research-based reports on changing global drug use patterns, assists UN–member countries in implementing international treaties, and provides technical assistance to countries in fighting drug use, drug trafficking, and other crime. In 1998, the UN General Assembly Special Session on drugs set as its goals "eliminating or significantly reducing the illicit cultivation of the coca bush, the cannabis plant and the opium poppy by the year 2008" and "achieving significant and measurable results in the field of demand reduction" (Nadelmann 2007:1).

The current international multibillion-dollar War on Drugs, sponsored and pushed by the U.S. and adopted by many other countries as well as by the drug control agencies of the UN, represents a dramatic and complex up-turn in a rather long line of international initiatives to control drugs. That drugs remain a significant global threat to health and development almost 100 years since the International Opium Convention suggests the continued failure of such programs (even if certain controls on certain drugs in certain times and places have diminished availability and use for varying periods of time) (Singer 2004).

Once it is established, it is evident that drug use is not easy to eradicate, although patterns change over time as do populations of users. The appeal of specific drugs waxes and wanes (in part, in response to popular experiences with using it, as well as in response to the appearance of new drugs or ways of using them), but drug use, in its many forms, continues. Thus, as Nadelmann observes, "global production and consumption of [the] drugs [the UN General Assembly

Special Session said it would eliminate or at least significantly control by 2008] are roughly the same as they were a decade ago; meanwhile, many producers have become more efficient, and cocaine and heroin have become purer and cheaper" (2007:1). Moreover, revelations over the years have shown that government and international efforts to control drugs often are colored by political motives that have little to do with curbing the harmful effects drugs might have on individuals, families, communities, or whole nations. With these issues in mind, we turn to an examination of the contemporary U.S.-led War on Drugs, especially to its international activities.

THE IMPACT OF THE U.S. WAR ON DRUGS ON DEVELOPING NATIONS

Drug Control USA

It is difficult to put a precise date on the beginning of the War on Drugs. While it is fair to say that the effort to control drug use in the U.S. dates to the early years of the twentieth century and to the passage of the Harrison Act, the actual degree of focus on drugs as a national public issue, however, has ebbed and flowed. Since the Korean War, however, there has been a consistent and growing federal effort to implement new policies and programs specifically designed to control drug use. These efforts significantly intensified in response to the radical increase in drug use, especially among youth and young adults, that began in the mid-1960s. As Musto comments, "The use of illegal drugs increased astoundingly in the 1960s. Drugs thought safely interred with the past, marijuana and heroin, rapidly resurfaced at the same time that new drugs such as LSD materialized and attained tremendous popularity" (1987:253). In response, in 1972, President Richard Nixon named drugs "public enemy number one" (cited in Chambers and Inciardi 1974:221) and declared an all-out war to eliminate unlawful drug use. Notes Musto, "No President has equaled Nixon's antagonism to drug abuse, and he took an active role in organizing the federal and state governments to fight the onslaught of substance abuse" (1987:254). While perhaps not equaled, Nixon's antidrug campaign established a precedent followed by every presidential administration ever since.

Yet, the story of U.S. drug control initiatives—and the ways in which subsequent presidents followed Nixon's lead—is far more complicated than at first glance. For example, although it has never been fully verified, investigative reporter Edward Epstein (1977) has argued that one of Nixon's primary motives in significantly expanding federal involvement in drug control, including the creation of various new governmental monitoring and control agencies (such as the Special Action Office for Drug Abuse Prevention, now called the White House Office of National Drug Control Policy, and the Drug Enforcement Administration), was the desire for a mechanism he could use to gather information on his political enemies (Singer 2006b). Moreover, in focusing on Turkey (instead of Southeast Asia) as the primary point of origin of most illicit heroin coming into the U.S. at the time, Browning and Garret (1986:123) argue:

> Nixon . . . ignored the real sources of narcotics trade abroad and by so doing . . . effectively precluded any possibility of being able to deal with heroin at home. It is he more than anyone else who ha[d] underwritten that trade through the policies he . . . formulated, the alliances he . . . forged, and . . . the political appointments he . . . made.

Of equal note, after the fall of the Shah of Iran in 1979, the CIA began to develop a growing presence in Afghanistan (on Iran's northern border), which was beginning to emerge as an important opium-producing area. CIA personnel forged alliances with opium-growing Baluchi and Pashtun peoples as a means of keeping an eye on (and a hand in) events in Iran. When the Soviet Union invaded Afghanistan in 1979, the CIA, at the request of President Jimmy Carter, began supplying arms and logistic support to the northern tribes. As a result of "high-powered CIA largess" and a record poppy crop in the region, there appeared a new "monster source of opium production [that] . . . promise[d] to send a veritable hurricane of heroin swirling once again through the streets of Europe and America: Afghanistan" (Levins 1986:125). Similarly, the program launched by the U.S. State Department's International Narcotics Control to eradicate opium production in Burma in the early 1970s was later found by investigators from the U.S. House Select Committee on Narcotics to have been primarily "a form of economic warfare aimed at subjugation of . . . Minority Peoples" (U.S. Congress 1977:225).

As these examples suggest, from early on the War on Drugs has had a very strong "supply-side" focus (i.e., on the countries in which drugs that reach the U.S. originate), which has been driven at least in part, or at times primarily, by the global geopolitical designs of U.S. foreign policy, rather than by a concern for the harmful effects of drug use. Further, Trentlage argues, "This supply-side focus may be explained by the scores of studies which pronounce the utter failure of domestic anti-drug policies such as the DARE program" (2006:84). Indeed, an increasingly recognized and disturbing consequence of U.S. domestic antidrug policies, is that the country

> ranks first in the world in per capita incarceration—with less than 5 percent of the world's population, but almost 25 percent of the

world's prisoners. The number of people locked up for U.S. drug-law violations has increased from roughly 50,000 in 1980 to almost 500,000 today; that's more than the number of people Western Europe locks up for everything. (Nadelmann 2007:4)

Disproportionately, prisoners of the War on Drugs are poor and members of disadvantaged ethnic minorities, including African Americans, Latinos, and Native Americans. Members of these socially and economically marginalized groups are significantly more likely to be stopped by the police for suspected drug violations (mostly possession), arrested on drug-related charges, serve more time behind bars for such offenses, and, as a result, suffer the stigmatizing effects of having a prison record, which, in and of itself, is an enduring barrier to improved socioeconomic status and hence a motive for continued self-medicating drug use (Singer 2007). This warehousing of the poor and people of color on drug charges occurs despite strong indications that it is more cost effective to fight drug abuse through investment in treatment than investment in incarceration (Rydell and Everingham 1994).

Globalizing the War on Drugs

The War on Drugs, however, is not solely a U.S. domestic affair. Rather, it is a global war carried out through various programs implemented in three world theaters of operation by the U.S. Bureau for International Narcotics and Law Enforcement Affairs (INL): the Andean program, which targets Colombia, Bolivia, and Peru; the Western Hemisphere program, aimed at Latin American and Caribbean countries; and the South Asia program, which focuses on Afghanistan and Pakistan. In these three regions, five different carrot-and-stick strategies are used to try and control drugs, as described below.

Eradication of Psychotropic Crops. To achieve this objective, the U.S. funds programs designed to fumigate poppy flowers, coca bushes, and marijuana plants with dangerous and environmentally damaging herbicides (e.g., Roundup Ultra) although other options, such as the use of biologically altered plant pathogens, also have been considered. In addition, these programs generally offer technical assistance in crop eradication, intelligence on targeted crop locations, aircraft to conduct aerial spraying, and related equipment and training to developing nations (Trentlage 2006). Exemplary of the problems with this approach is a program developed during the administration of President Bill Clinton called Plan Colombia, which was supported initially with a contribution of $1.3 billion in U.S. foreign aid (on top of an already considerable Colombian aid program) and the assistance of as many as 800 U.S. military and civilian personnel.

As originally conceived, Plan Colombia consisted of 55 percent military aid and 45 percent developmental aid, and called for the spraying of illicit cocoa farms. In the end, however, the program did little in the way of development and was primarily focused on fighting leftist rebels engaged in what at the time was a 50-year-old guerilla war against the Colombian government (Stokes 2005). According to Philadelphia journalist Ben Wallis-Wells (2007), who spent four months interviewing people involved in Plan Colombia, it is not completely clear why Clinton supported such a major escalation in the War on Drugs, but one factor may have been corporate interests:

> In early 2000, Clinton unveiled Plan Colombia—and Sikorksy [Aircraft Corp. of Connecticut] promptly received an order for eighteen of its Blackhawk helicopters at a cost of $15 million each. Plan Colombia would be the Clinton administration's primary and most costly contribution to the War on Drugs. But as with so many other aspects of American drug policy, the plan had an unintended consequence. . . . Colombia used the military aid to target the left-wing . . . even though many believed that right-wing paramilitaries, who were allies of the government, were more directly involved in narcotrafficking.

An additional goal of Plan Colombia may have been making the coca-growing region safe for oil exploration and extraction, as Colombia is a major supplier of oil to the U.S., and fumigation has focused on oil-producing areas even though coca is grown elsewhere in the Colombia as well (Cuellar 2005). As for the effect of the program on coca cultivation, while over 1,300 square kilometers of coca fields were sprayed in 2004, the planting of new areas resulted in little if any drop in coca production. Even so, the administration of President George W. Bush, which adopted Clinton's program, claiming that the "war against narco-terrorism can and will be won, and Colombia is well on its way to that victory," expanded Plan Colombia as part of his Andean Counterdrug Initiative (quoted in U.S. Department of State 2004). As a result, 20 aircraft—piloted by private contractors who work for DynCorp International—carry out daily spraying missions, while Colombian military units clear out local coca farmers (and guerilla fighters) and keep watch over cleared areas using a fleet of 71 U.S.–provided helicopters. Nonetheless, in its 2007 World Drug Report, the UN Office on Drugs and Crime concluded:

> In 2006, the area under coca cultivation in Bolivia, Colombia and Peru amounted to 156,900 ha. [1 hectare = 10,000 square meters or 2.471 acres]. While this represents a small decline of 2 per cent compared to 2005, the decrease in Colombia was almost entirely offset by increases in Bolivia and Peru. The cultivation estimates show that the global area under coca has been essentially stable since 2003. (2007b:65)

This pattern, sometimes referred to as the "balloon effect," consists of eradication pressure applied successfully in one locale leading to the rapid expansion of drug production in another locale. Additionally, eradication efforts have been criticized because they have not been coupled with effective programs for assisting small drug-crop farmers to adopt alternative livelihoods (e.g., such programs have been underfunded, not well managed, and characterized by top-down approaches), while environmentalists have expressed strong concern about the damage being done to the environment and the people who live in defoliated regions. According to Livingston (2004:123): "Plan Colombia has . . . harmed the health of thousands . . . and may cause irreparable damage to the Amazon rain forest. . . . Fumigation . . . is expected to create one million refugees."

Interdiction and Support of Foreign Law Enforcement. When it involves another country, U.S. drug interdiction efforts generally include providing funding, intelligence about drug operations, equipment, and personnel training (e.g., in surveillance, drug field-testing, intelligence collection, management skills, and basic law enforcement). This aid goes to military or law enforcement groups involved in targeting illicit drug corporations, their drug production and shipment activities, and their identified leaders. In assessing the effectiveness of these efforts in the case of Colombia, Trentlage observes that while a significant quantity of drugs is seized, "when the amounts of . . . interdicted cocaine are compared to the annual expenditures of the U.S. in the form of aid to Colombia the picture is rather bleak" (2004:94).

Moreover, apprehension has been aired about human rights violations being committed by foreign troops trained by the U.S. entities like the Drug Enforcement Administration in drug interdiction tactics. With reference to Latin America, for example, Wallis-Wells (2007) notes, "Those we are paying to wage the drug war have been accused of human-rights abuses in Peru, Bolivia and Colombia. In Mexico, we are now repeating many of the same mistakes we have made in the Andes." In the case of Mexico, human rights abuse by U.S.–trained drug control forces has included torture and the use of evidence in drug prosecutions that was obtained through the use of torture (Freeman and Sierra 2005). Similarly, in Bolivia, notes Amatangelo:

> Members of the U.S.-funded anti-drug police and the joint military/ police task force carry out massive anti-drug sweeps where hundreds of individuals may be detained at a time. The security forces systematically carry out arbitrary arrests, and Amnesty International has documented that detainees are frequently beaten or tortured while in detention and then later released. Arrests often deliberately target those individuals who are involved in union activity. Security forces are rarely held accountable for their actions. (2002:12)

The potential for antidrug military training to run counter to the goals of development, goals that include expanding human rights and strengthening human dignity, is considerable given that in recent years tens of thousands of foreign soldiers from over 180 countries have been trained by the U.S. (U.S. Department of State 2001). Federal funding for such programs has grown considerably despite a 1973 Congressional ban following revelations of significant human rights violations by U.S.-trained police in several developing countries. One way around this ban has been through the use of private military contractors. This development has drawn a strong negative reaction from some U.S. military personnel. In an essay for the Army War College, for example, Col. Bruce Grant observed that "privatization is a way of going around Congress and not telling the public. Foreign policy is made by default by private military consultants motivated by bottom-line profits" (quoted in Tamayo 2001:1).

Diplomatic Initiatives.   This strategy takes various forms but usually involves the U.S. using its wealth, might, and influence to bring nations to the War on Drugs planning table. For example, in February 1990, President George H. W. Bush called a summit between the U.S. and three South American nations deeply involved in the illicit cocaine trade: Colombia, Bolivia, and Peru. Noting flagging efforts to contain illicit cocaine corporations, the aim of the meeting was to keep these three nations enlisted in the War on Drugs by intensifying the battle against coca production. To entice compliance, the U.S. offered to provide $2.2 billion in economic and military aid (Harris 1991). Additionally, while most components of the international War on Drugs require some form of contract and collaboration with foreign governments and their police and military forces, building effective collaborative arrangements has been challenged by the weaknesses of law enforcement in many developing nations. More importantly, as the conservative Cato Institute stresses, in the War on Drugs the U.S. "has intruded into the complex social settings of dozens of countries around the globe by pressuring foreign governments to adopt laws and policies of its liking" (Vásquez 2002:567).

Use of Economic Sanctions or Restrictions on Foreign Aid.   This overtly coercive approach to drug control targets drug-producing countries that the U.S. determines are not cooperative with its antidrug initiatives. Following passage of a law by President Ronald Reagan in 1986, which made drug trafficking a national security issue, the federal government has identified the availability of a wide set of options in this regard, such as reducing or eliminating foreign aid, voting against multilateral development bank loans, stopping all preferential tariff benefits, increasing duties on imports to the U.S., and suspending airline transportation. In fact, geopolitical factors have shaped the sanctions agenda, and such measures have been imposed only on countries that have no relations or only severely strained relations with the U.S., rather than on those that are most extensively involved in drug production and trafficking (Sciolino 1989). For fiscal year 2007, the U.S. government designated Afghanistan, the Bahamas, Bolivia, Brazil, Colombia, the Dominican Republic, Ecuador, Guatemala, Haiti, India, Jamaica, Laos, Mexico, Myanmar, Nigeria, Pakistan, Panama, Paraguay, Peru, and Venezuela as major drug transit or illicit drug-producing countries but did not impose sanctions on them because they were close U.S. allies or because of fear of causing political destabilization that was determined not to be in the best interests of the U.S. (Office of the White House Press Secretary 2006).

Development of Domestic Institutions in Producer or Trafficker Countries. This approach, which tends not to be a standalone strategy but generally is linked to bilateral eradication and interdiction programs, involves assisting developing countries on strengthening their judicial and law enforcement infrastructures by basing them primarily on U.S. models. Two programs within the U.S. Department of Justice, for example the Office of Overseas Prosecutorial Development, Assistance and Training and the International Criminal Investigative Training Assistance Program, work with criminal justice bodies and police forces in developing countries throughout the world. Types of assistance include aiding in the implementation of public hearings, introducing cross-examination and live testimony, establishing mandatory minimal sentencing, use of electronic surveillance, and development of witness protection programs (Swartz 2001).

Military Force. Use of this strategy was most clearly illustrated in the U.S. invasion of Panama—under the code name "Operation Just Cause"—to arrest Manuel Noriega on money laundering and drug trafficking charges on December 20, 1989. The administration of President George H. W. Bush justified this military action, which involved the U.S. Army, Navy, Marines, and Armed National Guard, as a legal operation and a major victory in the War on Drugs. Despite the scale of the U.S. military effort, Noriega evaded capture and sought refuge in the Apostolic Nunciature, the Vatican's diplomatic mission in Panama City. Learning of his whereabouts, the U.S. turned to psychological warfare, including the round-the-clock playing of extremely loud rock-and-roll music from a perimeter set up around the mission property. In the end, Noriega surrendered and was immediately extradited to the U.S. for trial on an array of charges. Found guilty, he was sentenced ultimately to 30 years of incarceration in the federal prison in Miami and remains there as a prisoner of war under the terms of the Geneva Convention.

It has been broadly documented (Dinges 1991, Scott and Marshall 1991) that for over a decade, and long after it was known he was involved in drug trafficking, Noriega was on the payroll of the CIA. In this role, among other chores, Noriega facilitated the flow of illegal "guns-for-drugs" aid to the counterrevolutionary contras as they attempted, with U.S. backing, to overthrow the Sandinista government in Nicaragua. Loss of trust in Noriega among U.S. officials was triggered by the discovery that he also was selling intelligence and other services to the Cuban and Sandinista governments.

According to the White House, casualties of the invasion were low, including 200 Panamanians and 29 U.S. soldiers. The New York–based Center for Constitutional Rights, however, on behalf of 300 victims of the invasion, brought a lawsuit claiming there were actually more than 2,000 people killed and that the attack left 20,000 people homeless and damages that exceeded $2 billion. Even higher estimates of Panamanian causalities have been reported. On December 29, 1989, the UN General Assembly voted 75–20 with 40 abstentions to condemn the invasion as a flagrant violation of international law (International Development Research Centre 2001). In 2007, Panama's legislature declared the anniversary of the U.S. invasion a day of national mourning, reflecting popular sentiment that the event was a blow to national pride. According to Cesar Pardo, a member of the legislature, "This is a recognition of those who fell . . . as a result of the cruel and unjust invasion by the most powerful army in the world" (quoted in Zamorano 2007:1).

An especially violent expression of the War on Drugs was launched by the Thaksin Shinawatra government in Thailand in February 2003. During the initial phase of this program, the country recorded over 2,000 extrajudicial killings. While the government blamed these deaths on groups involved in the drug trade, Human Rights Watch (Cohen 2004) and other human rights organizations revealed that they were caused by a draconian government crackdown on drug users implemented by the Thai police. This campaign did not end illegal drug use in Thailand, but it did make it far more dangerous while eroding human rights and promoting the spread of HIV among terrified drug users and incarcerated individuals. The U.S. bestowed its blessing on Thailand's War on Drugs in June of 2003 when Prime Minister Thaksin visited the White House, which subsequently issued a press release praising Thaksin's war on drug trafficking (The White House 2003).

The War on Drugs and the Struggle for Development

How has the War on Drugs impacted underdeveloped countries? Review of the research suggests two conclusions: (1) the War on Drugs has not achieved its primary objective of reducing the production and flow of illicit drugs in developing countries nor has it reduced the movement or purity of these drugs into the U.S. or elsewhere; and (2) the War on Drugs has inflicted a considerable amount of collateral damage on developing countries, including undermining civic society, threatening democracy and civil liberties, and violating human rights and dignity.

Regarding the first point, summarizing a range of assessments by various scholars and policy bodies, Trentlage succinctly concludes that "efforts to halt international production of illegal substances and transit of such substances to American markets have largely resulted in failure" (2006:85). Similarly, notes Vásquez, the international War on Drugs has "failed by every measure. . . . [Further, it has] severely aggravate[ed] political, economic, and social problems in developing countries" (2002:575).

As for the second point, in many developing countries the War on Drugs has undercut civil liberties and human rights, strengthened the armed forces in countries with a history of harsh military rule, supported militarization of local police forces, spread the use of torture by law enforcement, provided support to powerful leaders who are themselves heavily implicated in the drug trade, contributed to a significant social conflict and political instability, and undercut the livelihood of impoverished people without providing them with alternative means of making a living (Youngers and Rosin 2004). As Jay Olson of the Washington Office on Latin America (WALO) stresses with reference to the region of concern to his organization, "U.S. drug-control efforts have provoked a war on the poor and an assault on democratic institutions. . . . We've spent billions on anti-drug efforts in Latin America and have nothing to show for it but collateral damage" (quoted in Lobe 2004).

For these reasons, the War on Drugs has been labeled a "failed policy" by many observers. In part, this failure is a product of the politicization of the drug control agenda: namely, a consistent pattern of using the issues of drug production and trafficking to address other, often narrow and self-interested, political and economic goals, including political domination and corporate economic exploitation. In light of the considerable damage that legal and illegal drugs have on the lives of people and processes of development, it is evident that an alternative approach is needed, one that in developing nations focuses on promoting human rights and enhancing human dignity while it strengthens "democratic institutions, the rule of law . . . and police accountability . . . and offers viable alternatives to impoverished rural farmers and to marginalized and alienated urban youth" (Neild 2004:93).

TOWARD ALTERNATIVE APPROACHES

In exploring alternative approaches to the issue of drugs and development, it is important to recognize that the contemporary development discourse is inherently paradoxical. This paradox emerges from the fact that it is the very countries (e.g., Western European nations, the United States, and Japan) that epitomize advanced development in the modern world that have instigated the human rights–destroying processes of colonialism, economic exploitation, environmental degradation, international conflict, and globalism, which have promoted the development of underdeveloped. In other words, in discussions of development and drug-related issues, it is necessary to pay close attention to the role of power, both in terms of political and economic might and ideological dominance. With reference to the latter, the Italian political theorist Antonio Gramsci (1971) introduced the notion of "cultural hegemony," which refers to the tendency of dominated groups to absorb the terms and worldviews of their dominators. Thus, one of the essential features of globalism is the hegemonic dissemination of First World concepts and understandings of development into Third World experiences and aspirations, a transformation that began with colonial administration and continues today with the sweeping rush of global information and communication technology. Notably, Gramsci stressed that counterhegemonic strategy—such as the forging of rights and dignity-centered approaches to development—must involve dominated groups creating cultures of their own that are independent of the self-interested ideas promulgated by dominant social groups in the world.

As we have seen, much of drug control policy historically has been driven by an interest-based agenda controlled by those with the power to set global policy. Several interests have been in play in the development domain, including those of dominant nations seeking to maintain or expand economic and political advantage in global competition, corporations in search of opportunities for global position and sales, and government officials attempting to advance their personal political agendas. The consequence has been the development of drug control policies and programs that not only have failed in their stated missions but have contributed to the total sum of social suffering and repressive social control in the world. To move beyond the current morass, there is a critical need, therefore, for a shift from narrow interest-based to vigorous evidence-based approaches for responding to the negative effects of drug use and trafficking, with the objective of expanding the quality of life, the centrality of justice, and the quotient of human dignity in the world. Importantly, evidence-based policy and program development have been shown to contribute to more successful and acceptable outcomes suggesting that the promises of beneficial social change can be kept (Cernea 1995, Chambers 1991, Rew 1997).

An evidence-based approach to drugs and development that is unencumbered by the self-serving political and economic interests of developed nations would allow a thoughtful review of issues like drug legalization that currently are ruled out by antidrug warriors. Further, it would support careful policy consideration of the implications of research findings showing that: legal drugs inflict more human harm than illegal ones; investment in drug treatment is more cost effective than supply-side actions like interdiction and arrest; there are important health benefits for the whole population of harm reduction approaches to drug use; self-medicating drug use is rooted in health and social disparities not inherent criminality; and there are distressing negative effects of the policies of the War on Drugs on developing countries (and subordinated strata of developed countries as well).

All of these issues are of concern to a growing body of increasingly linked grassroots nongovernment organizations, or what Keck and Sikkink (1997) have called "transnational activist networks." Building the capacity within networks of organizations embedded in local communities in developing nations to "set goals, achieve expertise, share knowledge, and generate commitment" (Appadurai, 2006:134), as well as to avoid externally imposed norms and expectations (Escobar 1995) offers a meaningful alternative to the negative effects of drugs and existing antidrug efforts in development.

References

Abel, E. 1982. *Marijuana: The First Twelve Thousand Years*. New York: McGraw-Hill.

Agbavon, P. 2001. The Tobacco Industry and Tobacco Control Movement in Togo. Online at: http://www.essentialaction.org/tobacco/qofm/0201/togo.html (accessed 7/22/06).

Achebe, C. 1984. *The Trouble with Nigeria*. London: Heineman Educational Books.

Amadi, S. 2007. Colonial Legacy, Elite Dissension and the Making of Genocide: The Story of Biafra. Online at: http://howgenocidesend.ssrc.org/Amadi (accessed 11/25/07).

Amatangelo, G. 2002. "Moving Beyond the 'War on Drugs': Drugs, Democracy, and the Andean Crisis." Presented at the Drug Policy Conference, Rice University, April 10–11.

Amir, S. 2006. "The Millennium Development Goals: A Critique from the South." *Monthly Review* 57(10). Online at: http://www.monthlyreview.org/0306amin2.htm (accessed 10/12/06).

Anderson, B. 2006. *Imagined Communities*. London: Verso.

Andreas, P. 1995. "Free Market Reform and Drug Market Prohibition: U.S. Policies at Cross-Purposes in Latin America." *Third World Quarterly* 16(1):75–87.

Andreas, P. 2004. Illicit International Political Economy: The Clandestine Side of Globalization. *Review of International Political Economy* 11(3):641–652.

Andreas, P. and Nadelmann, E. 2006. *Policing the Globe: Criminalization and Crime Control in International Relations*. Oxford: Oxford University Press.

Appadurai, A., Ed. 1986. "Introduction: Commodities and the Politics of Value." In *The Social Life of Things: Commodities in Cultural Perspective*. Cambridge: Cambridge University Press.

Appadurai, A. 2006. *Fear of Small Numbers*. Durham, NC: Duke University Press.

Arias, E. 2006. *Drugs & Democracy in Rio de Janeiro: Trafficking, Social Networks and Public Security*. Chapel Hill: University of North Carolina Press.

Ash, L. 2006. "Hard Return for Jamaica Drugs Mule." *BBC News*, January 19. Online at: http://news.bbc.co.uk/1/hi/world/americas/4629282.stm (accessed 11/20/07).

Asian Human Rights Commission and People's Vigilance Committee for Human Rights. 2006. INDIA: Human Dignity Is the True Measure of Development. Online at: http://www.ahrchk.net/statements/mainfile.php/2006statements/661 (accessed 11/23/07).

Avalon Project.1997. Inaugural Address of Harry S. Truman. Yale School of Law. Online at: http://www.yale.edu/lawweb/avalon/presiden/inaug/truman.htm (accessed 12/2/06).

Baer, H., Singer, M. and Susser, I. 2003. *Medical Anthropology and the World System*, 2nd edition. West Port, CT: Bergin and Garvey.

Baran, P. 1962. *The Political Economy of Growth*. New York: Monthly Review Press.

Barker, K. 2006. "'Very Bad' News on Opium War." *Chicago Tribune*, September 3, p. 1.

Barnet, R. and Cavanagh, J. 1994. *Global Dreams: Imperial Corporations and the New World Order*. New York: Simon and Schuster.

Battin, M., Luna, E., Lipman, A., Gahlinger, P. and Rollins, D. 2008. *Drugs and Justice: Seeking a Consistent, Coherent, Comprehensive View*. Oxford: Oxford University Press.

Bayer, I, and Ghodse, H. 1999. "Evolution of International Drug Control, 1945–1995." *Bulletin of Narcotics* 51(1 and 2).

BBC News. 2002. "Ex-BBC Journalist Killed in Jamaica." June 9. Online at: http://news.bbc.co.uk/1/hi/world/americas/2032605.stm (accessed 11/20/07).

Benedict, C. 1996. *Bubonic Plague in Nineteenth-century China*. Stanford, CA: Stanford University Press.

Black, R. and White, H. 2004. *Targeting Development: Critical Perspectives on the Millennium Development Goals*. London: Routledge.

Bonnie, R. and Whitebread, C. 1970. "The Forbidden Fruit and the Tree of Knowledge: An Inquiry into the Legal History of American Marijuana Prohibition." *Virginia Law Review* 56(6):971–1203.

Boonwaat, L. 2006. "Opium Elimination in Laos: Poverty Alleviation and Development Challenges." Illicit Special Issue on Drugs and Development. *Development Bulletin* 69:52–55.

Bordes, A. 1979. *Évolution des Sciences de la Santé et de l'Hygiène Publique en Haiti*. Tome 1. Port-au-Prince: Centre d' Higiene Familiale.

Bose, S. 2007. *Contested Lands*. Cambridge, MA: Harvard.

Boyce-Reid, K. 1995. The Challenge for Women with a Drug-abusing Family Member: The Jamaican Perspective. Online at: http://www.unodc.org/unodc/bulletin/bulletin_1995-01-01_1_page005.html (accessed 11/20/07).

Browning, F. and Garrett, B. 1986. "The CIA and the New Opium War." In *Culture and Politics of Drugs*, P. Park and W. Matveychuk, eds., pp. 118–124. Dubuque, IA: Kendall/Hunt.

Calvani, S., Guia, E. and Lemahieu, J-L. 1997. "Drug Resistance Rating: An Innovative Approach for Measuring a Country's Capacity to Resist Illegal Drugs." *Third World Quarterly* 18(4):659–672.

Center for Public Integrity. 2001. Tobacco Companies Linked to Criminal Organizations in Cigarette Smuggling. Online at: http://www.publici.org/report.aspx?aid=353 (accessed 7/12/06).

Central Eurasia Project. 2003. Drug Trafficking Emerges as Top National Security Threat to Tajikistan. On line at: http://www.eurasianet.org/departments/insight/articles/eav050803.shtml (accessed 11/22/07).

Central Intelligence Agency (CIA). 2007. Guyana. World Factbook. Online at: https://www.cia.gov/search?NS-search-page=document&NS-rel-doc-name=/library/publications/the-world-factbook/print/gy.html&NS-query=Guyana&NS-search-type=NS-boolean-query&NS-collection=Everything&NS-docs-found=920&NS-doc-number=1 (accessed 11/20/07).

Cernea, M. 1995. "Social Organization and Development Anthropology. Environmentally Sustainable Development." *Studies and Monographs Series*, no. 6. Washington, DC: World Bank.

Chambers, C. and Inciardi, J. 1974. "Forecasts for the Future: Where We Are and Where We Are Going." In *Drugs and the Criminal Justice System*, J. Inciardi and C. Chambers, eds. Beverly Hills, CA: Sage.

Chambers, R. 1991. "Shortcut and Participatory Methods for Gaining Social Information for Projects." In *Putting People First: Sociological Variables in Rural Development*, 2nd edition. M. M. Cernea, ed, pp. 515–537. New York: Oxford University Press for the World Bank.

Chandarpal, N. 2000. Statement to the Twenty-Fourth Special Session of the General Assembly, World Summit for Social Development and Beyond: Achieving Social Development for all in a Globalising World. Online at: http://www.un.org/socialsummit/speeches/306guy.htm (accessed 11/25/07).

Clawson, P. and Lee, R. 1998. *The Andean Cocaine Industry*. New York: St. Martin's Griffin.

Cohen, J. 2004. "Not Enough Graves: The War on Drugs, HIV/AIDS, and Violations of Human Rights." *Human Rights Watch* 16(8):1–58.

Cohen, P. 2006. "Help as Threat: Alternative Development and the 'War on Drugs.'" *Development Bulletin* 69:31–35.

Cohen, P. 2008. "Preface." In *Drugs and Justice: Seeking a Consistent, Coherent, Comprehensive View*, Margaret Battin, Erik Luna, Arthur Lipman, Paul Gahlinger and Douglas Rollins, eds., pp. v–xvi. Oxford: Oxford University Press.

Commission of Inquiry. 1984. Report of the Commission of Inquiry Appointed to Inquire into the Illegal Use of the Bahamas for the Transshipment of Dangerous Drugs Destined for the United States of America, October 1983–December 1984. Nassau, Bahamas.

Conrad, P. and Schneider, J. 1980. *Deviance and Medicalization: From Badness to Sickness*. St. Louis: C. V. Mosby.

Constable, P. 2002. "In Tajikistan, a Gateway for Heroin." *Washington Post*, July 26. Online at: http://www.hartford-hwp.com/archives/53/155.html (accessed 11/26/07).

Coomber, R. and South, N., Eds. 2004. *Drug Use and Cultural Contexts "Beyond the West."* London: Free Association Books.

Cubillos-Garzon, L., Casas, J., Morillo, C. and Bautista, L. 2004. "Congestive Heart Failure in Latin America: The Next Epidemic." *American Heart Journal* 47(3):386–389.

Cuellar, F. 2005. *The Profits of Extermination: How U.S. Corporate Power is Destroying Colombia*. Monroe, ME: Common Courage Press.

Davis, C. 2000. "Tajikistan's Battle with Addiction." *BBC News*, June 6. Online at: http://news.bbc.co.uk/1/hi/world/asia-pacific/774769.stm (accessed 11/25/07).

de Queiroz, M. 2007. "Guinea-Bissau: African Paradise for South American Traffickers." *IPS News*, August 27. Online at: http://ipsnews.net/news.asp?idnews=38857 (accessed 12/2/07).

de Souza, J. and Urani, A. 2002. *Children in Drug Trafficking: A Rapid Assessment*. Geneva: International Labor Organization.

Department of Economic and Social Affairs of the United Nations. 2006. *Millennium Development Goals Report*. Vienna, Austria: Vienna International Centre.

Destrebecq, D. and Leggett, T. 2007. *Cocaine Trafficking in West Africa: The Threat to Stability and Development* (with Special Reference to Guinea-Bissau). Bratislava, Slovakia: United Nations Office on Drugs and Crime.

Devaney, M., Reid, G. and Baldwin, S. 2005. *Situational Analysis of Illicit Drug Issues and Responses in the Asia-Pacific Region*. Sydney: Australian National Council on Drugs.

Dinges, J. 1991. *Our Man in Panama*. New York: Random House.

Drug Policy Alliance. 2007a. Race and the Drug War: History of Prohibition. Online at: http://www.drugpolicy.org/communities/race/historyofpro.

Drug Policy Alliance. 2007b. UNGASS: International Control of Marijuana. Online at: http://www.drugpolicy.org/global/ungass/marijuana (accessed 9/22/07).

Duiker, W. 2000. *Ho Chi Minh—A Life*. New York: Hyperion.

Dumarest, J. 1938. Les Monopoles de l'Opium et du Sel en Indochine. Ph.D. Thesis. University de Lyon.

Epstein, E. 1977. *Agency of Fear*. New York: G.P. Putnam's.

Erlen, J. and Spillane, J., Eds. 2004. *Federal Drug Control: The Evolution of Policy and Practice*. New York: The Hawthorn Press.

Escobar, A. 1995. *Encountering Development: The Making and Unmaking of the Third World*. Princeton: Princeton University Press.

EuropaWorld. 2002. Impact of Illicit Drugs on Economic Development Focus of UN Expert Panel Meeting. Online at: http://www.europaworld.org/week104/impactofillicit81102.htm (accessed 11/20/07).

Farmer, P. 1999. *Infections and Inequalities: The Modern Plagues*. Berkeley: University of California Press.

Farmer, P. and Bertrand, D. 2000. "Hypocrisies of Development and the Health of the Haitian Poor." In *Dying for Growth: Global Inequality and the Health of the Poor*, Jim Yong Kim, Joyce Millen, Alex Irwin and John Gershman, eds., pp. 65–90. Monroe, MA: Common Courage Press.

Farrell, G. and Thorne, J. 2005. "Where Have all the Flowers Gone?: Evaluation of the Taliban Crackdown against Opium Poppy." *International Journal of Drug Policy* 16:81–91.

Forero, J. and Weiner, T. 2002. "Latin American Poppy Fields Undermine U.S. Drug Battle." *New York Times*, June 8, p. 1.

Forward Thinking on Drug Use. 2003. A Review of UN Progress in Combating the Global Drug Problem. On line at: http://www.forward-thinking-on-drugs.org/index.html (accessed 10/8/06).

Founou-Tchuigoua, B. 2002. NEPAD or the Challenge to Catch Up. Presented at the African Scholars' Forum Meeting, Nairobi, Kenya, April 26–28.

Frank, A. G. 1966 (1989 reprint). "The Development of Underdevelopment." *Monthly Review* 18. Online at: http://findarticles.com/p/articles/mi_m1132/is_n2_v41/ai_7659725 (accessed 7/17/07).

Frank, A. G. 1991. The Underdevelopment of Development: From a Personal Preface to the Author's Intentions. Online at: http://www.druckversion.studien-von-zeitfragen.net/The%20Underdevelopment%20of%20Development.htm (accessed 7/17/07).

Fratello, S. 2001. "Falls from Paradise: Guyana's Kaieteur Falls is a Remote Yet Accessible Wilderness—This Land." *Natural History* (December). Online at: http://findarticles.com/p/articles/mi_m1134/is_10_110/ai_80774382 (accessed 11/22/07).

Freeman, L. and Sierra, J. 2005. "Mexico: The Militarization Trap." In *Drugs and Democracy in Latin America: The Impact of U.S. Policy*, Coletta Youngers and Eileen Rosin, eds, pp. 263–302. Boulder, CO: Lynne Rienner Publishers.

French, G. 2006. "Corruption in Guyana Perceived Rampant, Says Transparency Int'l." *Caribbean Net News*. Online at: http://webmail.aol.com/29047/aol/en-us/Suite.aspx (accessed 11/20/07).

FRONTLINE. 2000. "Drug Wars." Online at: http://www.pbs.org/wgbh/pages/frontline/shows/drugs/interviews/ochoajorge.html (accessed 5/6/06).

Fukuda-Parr, S. 2004. "The Millennium Development Goals: The Pledge of World Leaders to End Poverty Will Not Be Met with Business as Usual." *Journal of International Development* 16(7):925–932.

Ganguly, K. 2004. "Opium Use in Rajatham India: A Socio-Cultural Perspective." In *Drug Use and Cultural Contexts "Beyond the West,"* Ross Coomber and Nigel South, eds., pp 83–100. London: Free Association Books.

Gershman, J., and Irwin, A. 2000. "Getting a Grip on the Global Economy." In *Dying for Growth: Global Inequality and the Health of the Poor*, Jim Yong Kim, Joyce Millen, Alex Irwin and John Gershman, eds., pp. 11–43. Monroe, MA: Common Courage Press.

Global Health Watch. 2006. *Global Health Watch 2005–2006: An Alternative World Health Report*. London: Zed Books.

Global Partnerships for Tobacco Control. 2002. What Is Big Tobacco Up to Around the World? On line at: http://www.essentialaction.org/tobacco/qofm/0201a.html (accessed 7/21/06).

Goode, E. 1984. *Drugs in American Society*. New York: Doubleday Anchor.

Gramsci, A. 1971. *Selections from the Prison Notebooks*. London: Lawrence and Wishart.

Grant, C. 2002. "Jamaica: The New Wild West." *BBC News*, August 10. Online at: http://news.bbc.co.uk/1/hi/programmes/from_our_own_correspondent/2168229.stm (accessed 8/9/07).

Greste, P. 2000. "Haiti: "Weak Link" in Drug Chain." *BBC News*, May 16. Online at: http://news.bbc.co.uk/1/hi/world/americas/750434.stm (accessed 11/16/06).

Griffiths, P. 2006. "A Shot in the Arm: Transboundary Flows and Opiate Transition in Vietnam." *Development Bulletin* 66:59–63.

Grund, J.-P. 2004. "Harm Reduction for Poppy Farmers in Myanmar?" *Asian Harm Reduction Network*. Newsletter Issue 34:1–3.

Hanrahan, C. 2002. "Marijuana." In *Gale Encyclopedia of Alternative Medicine*, Jacqueline Longe, ed. Farmington Hills, MI: Gale Cengage.

Harris, J. 1991. *Drugged America*. New York: Four Winds Press.

Health, D. 1958. "Drinking Patterns of the Bolivian Camba." *Quarterly Journal of Studies on Alcohol*, 19:491–508.

Health, D. 1991. "Continuity and Change in Drinking Patterns of the Bolivian Camba." In *Society, Culture and Drinking Patterns Reexamined*, D. Pittman and H. White, eds. New Brunswick, NJ: Rutgers Center of Alcohol Studies.

Health, D. 2004. "Camba (Bolivia) Drinking Patterns: Changes in Alcohol Use, Anthropology and Research Perspectives." In *Drug Use and Cultural Contexts "Beyond the West,"* Ross Coomber and Nigel South, eds., pp 119–136. London: Free Association Books.

Henry-Lee, A. 2005. *Women in Prison: The Impact of the Incarceration of Jamaican women on Themselves and their Families*. Grenada Way, Jamaica: Planning Institute of Jamaica.

Herzfeld, M. 2005. *Cultural Intimacy: Social Poetics in the Nation-State*. New York: Routledge.

Hotez, P. 2003. *The Hookworm Vaccine Initiative*. Washington, DC: Sabin Vaccine Institute, Georgetown University.

Howell, S. 2003. "The Diffusion of Moral Values in a Global Perspective." In *Globalisation: Studies in Anthropology*, Thomas Hylland Eriksen, ed., pp. 198–216. London: Pluto Press.

Human Rights Watch. 2006. Haiti: Secure and Credible Elections Crucial for Stability. Online at: http://hrw.org/english/docs/2006/02/06/haiti12611_txt.htm (accessed 10/19/07).

Ibeanu, O. and Luckham, R. 2007. "'Nigeria': Political Violence, Governance, and Corporate Responsibility in a Petro-State." In *Oil Wars*, Mary Kaldor, Terry Lynn and Saih Yahia, eds., pp. 41–99. London: Pluto Press.

International Development Research Centre. 2001. *Responsibility to Protect*. Ottawa, Canada: International Commission on Intervention and State Sovereignty.

International Labor Organization. 1994. *A Training Handbook on Prevention of Alcohol and Drug Problems in the Maritime Sector*. Manila, Philippines: National Maritime Polytechnic.

Isbister, J. 2006. *Promises Not Kept: Poverty and the Betrayal of Third World Development*. Bloomfield, CT: Kumarian Press.

Ismi, A. 2002. Drugs and Corruption in North and South America. Canadian Centre for Policy Alternatives. Online at: http://141.117.225.2/~asadismi/drugscorruption.html (accessed 9/19/07).

Jankowiak, W. and Bradburd, D., Eds. 2003. *Drugs, Labor, and Colonial Expansion*. Tucson: University of Arizona Press.

Jelsma, M. 2005. "Learning Lessons from the Taliban Opium Ban." *International Journal on Drug Policy*, 16(2):1–8.

Jok, M. J. 2007. *Sudan: Race, Religion and Violence*. Oxford: Oneworld.

Kaldor, M., Lynn, T. and Yahia, S. 2007. "Introduction." In *Oil Wars*, Mary Kaldor, Terry Lynn and Saih Yahia, eds., pp. 1–40. London: Pluto Press.

Kavan, J. 2003. UN Information Service. Online at: http://www.unis.unvienna.org/unis/pressrels/2003/gasm322.html (accessed 11/20/07).

Keck, M. and Sikkink, K. 1997. *Activists Beyond Borders: Advocacy Networks in International Politics*. Ithaca, NY: Cornell University Press.

Kittrie, N. 1971. *The Right to Be Different*. Baltimore: Johns Hopkins University Press.

Lang, E. 2004. "Drugs and Society: A Social History." In *Drug Use in Australia*, Margaret Hamilton, Trevor King, and Alison Ritter, eds, pp. 1–13. Melbourne: Oxford University Press.

LeClézio, V. 2002. Tobacco Industry Activities in Mauritius. Online at: http://www.essentialaction.org/tobacco/qofm/0201/mauritius.html (accessed 6/22/06).

Levins, H. 1986. "The Shifting Source of Opium." In *Culture and Politics of Drugs*, P. Park and W. Matveychuk, eds., pp. 124–125. Dubuque, IA: Kendall/Hunt.

Levy, B. and Sidel, V. 2006. *Social Injustice and Health*. Oxford: Oxford University Press.

Livingston, G. 2004. *Inside Colombia: Drugs, Democracy and War*. New Brunswick, NJ: Rutgers University Press.

Lobe, J. 2004. "25-Year 'War on Drugs' Gets a Failing Grade." *Finalcall.com News*. Online at: http://www.finalcall.com/artman/publish/article_1699.shtml (accessed 12/12/07).

Lyttleton, C. 2006. "Opiates to Amphetamines: Development and Change in the Golden Triangle." *Development Bulletin* 69:22–26.

Mar, P. 1996. Medieval Sourcebook: Christopher Columbus: Extracts from Journal. Online at: http://www.fordham.edu/halsall/source/columbus1.html (accessed 1/3/08).

Marshall, D. 2001. Statement before the Senate Caucus on International Narcotics Control, May 15. Online at: http://www.usdoj.gov/dea/pubs/cngrtest/ct051501.htm (accessed 5/8/06).

Maternowska, M. C. 2006. *Reproducing Inequalities: Poverty and the Politics of Population in Haiti*. New Brunswick, NJ: Rutgers University Press.

McCoy, A. 1991. *The Politics of Heroin*. Brooklyn: Lawrence Hill.

Meredith, M. 1984. *The First Dance of Freedom: Black Africa in the Post-war Era*. New York: Harper & Row.

Mesquita, F. 2006. "The Health and Social Impacts of Drugs in Brazil and Indonesia: What It Means for Development." *Development Bulletin* 69:64–66.

Milford, J. 1997. Statement before the House Internal Relations Committee regarding Haiti, December 9. Online at: http://www.usdoj.gov/dea/pubs/cngrtest/ct971209.htm#THE%20TOLL%20OF%20THE%20DRUG%20TRADE%20IN%20HAITI (accessed 10/19/07).

Miller, J. 2007. "Drug Barons Turn Bissau into Africa's First Narco-State." *The Independent*, August 27, p. 1.

Minh, H. C. 1920. Collection of Letters by Ho Chi Minh. Online at: http://rationalrevolution.net/war/collection_of_letters_by_ho_chi_.htm (accessed 7/17/07).

Minh, H. C. 1961. *Selected Works*. Hanoi: Foreign Languages Publishing House.

Minh, H. C. 1967. *On Revolution: Selected Writings*, 1920–66. New York: Frederick A. Praeger.

Mintz, S. 1985. *Sweetness and Power: The Place of Sugar in Modern History*. New York: Penguin Books

Moreira, M. 2000. Not Soldiers, Not Innocents: Youth and Drug Trafficking in the City of Rio de Janeiro. Dissertation in Public Health. Rio de Janeiro, Brazil: Oswaldo Cruz Foundation.

Mozingo, J. 2005. "Horrors Persist in Forsaken Haitian Slum." *Miami Herald*, May 31. Online at: http://gangresearch.net/GangResearch/Media/aristidegangs.htm (accessed 10/19/07).

Muralidhar, S. 2007. "Gangs of Port-au-Prince." *The American Prospect*, July 11. Online at: http://www.prospect.org/cs/articles?article=gangs_of_portauprince (accessed 10/19/07).

Musto, D. 1987. *The American Disease: Origins of Narcotic Control*. Oxford: Oxford University Press.

Nadelmann, E. 2007. "Think Again: Drugs." *Foreign Policy*, September/October. Online at: http://www.foreignpolicy.com/story/cms.php?story_id=3932 (accessed 1/31/07).

Naval Intelligence. 1943. *Indochina*. Cambridge, England: Naval Intelligence.

Navarro, V. 2001. *The Political Economy of Social Inequalities: Consequences for Health and Quality of Life*. Amityville, NY: Baywood.

Neild, R. 2004., "U.S. Police Assistance and Drug Control Policies." In *Drugs and Democracy in Latin America: The Impact of U.S. Policy*, Coletta Youngers and Eileen Rosin, eds, pp. 61–98. Boulder, CO: Lynne Rienner Publishers.

Neville, M. and Clark, N. 1985. "Drug Abuse in the Bahamas." *Journal of Substance Abuse Treatment*, 2(3):195–197.

Nichter, M. and Cartwright, E. 1991. "Saving the Children for the Tobacco Industry." *Medical Anthropology* 5:236–256.

Office of the White House Press Secretary. 2006. White House Press Release: Memorandum for the Secretary of State: Presidential Determination on Major Drug Transit or Major Illicit Drug Producing Countries for Fiscal Year 2007. Presidential Determination No. 2006-24, September 15.

Osmonaliev, K. 2006. Interrelationship between Drug-Trafficking and Corruption in Central Asia. Presented at the Social Research Center, American University Central Asia, Bishkek, Kyrgyzstan, March 16. Online at: http://src.auca.kg/images/stories/files/report-Osmonaliev-english.pdf (accessed 12/13/07).

PakTribune. 2006. "Heroin Lab Workers Suffering from Different Diseases." Pakistan News Service, July 16.

Patten, C. 2001. "Never the Twain Shall Meet? Adapting Kipling to a Globalised World." *External Relations*. Online at: http://ec.europa.eu/external_relations/Patten/sp01-461.htm (accessed 1/25/08).

Polgreen, L. 2006. "Oil Riches Bring Blood to Nigerian Villagers." *New York Times*, p. 1.

Ranson, K., Poletti, T., Bornemisza, O. and Sondorp, E. 2007. *Promoting Health Equity in Conflict-Affected Fragile States*. Geneva: World Health Organization.

Razak, M., Jittiwutikarn, J., Suiyanon, V., Vongchuk, T., Srirak, J. and Beyer, C. 2003. "HIV Prevalence and Risks among Injection and Noninjection Drug Users in Northern Thailand: Need for Comprehensive HIV Prevention Programs." *Journal of Acquired Immune Deficiency Syndromes*, 33:259–266.

Reid, G. and Costigan, G. 2002. *Revisiting the "Hidden Epidemic": A Situational Analysis of Drug Use in Asia in the Context of HIV/AIDS*. Melbourne: Burnet Institute, Centre for Harm Reduction.

Revol, D. 2006. "Hoping for Change in Haiti's Cité-Soleil." *The Magazine of the International Red Cross and Red Crescent Movement*. Online at: http://www.redcross.int/EN/mag/magazine2006_2/10-11.html (accessed 11/22/07).

Rew, A. 1997. "The Donors' Discourse: Official Social Development Knowledge in the 1980s." In *Discourses of Development: Anthropological Perspectives*, R. D. Grillo and R. L. Stirrat, eds., pp. 81–106. Oxford: Berg.

Robinson, R. 1996. *The Great Book of Hemp: The Complete Guide to the Environmental, Commercial, and Medicinal Uses of the World's Most Extraordinary Plant*. Rochester, VT: Park Street Press.

Rydell, P. and Everingham, S. 1994. *Controlling Cocaine: Supply versus Demand Programs*. Santa Monica, CA: The Rand Corporation.

Rylko-Bauer, B., Singer, M. and van Willigin, J. 2006. "Reclaiming Applied Anthropology: Its Past, Present, and Future." *American Anthropologist* 108(1):178–190.

Schiray, M. and Fabre, G. 2002. *Globalisation, Drugs and Criminalisation: Final Report on Brazil, China, India and Mexico*. Paris: United Nations Educational, Scientific and Cultural Organisation.

Sciolino, E. 1989. "Drug Production Rising Worldwide State Dept. Says." *New York Times*, March 2, p. 1.

Scott, P. and Marshall, J. 1991. *Cocaine Politics: Drugs, Armies, and the CIA in Central America*. Berkeley: University of California Press.

Scott-Clark, C. and Levy, A. 2002. *The Stone of Heaven: Unearthing the Secret History of Imperial Green Jade*. London: Little Brown.

Seabrook, J. 1999. Smoking and the Poor. Third World Network. Online at: http://pnews.org/art/2art/tobacpoor.html (accessed 3/21/06).

Seecoomar, J. 2002. *Contributions toward the Resolution of Conflict in Guyana*. Leeds, UK: Peepal Tree Press.

Shishkin, P. and Crawford, D. 2006. "In Afghanistan, Heroin Trade Soars Despite U.S. Aid." *Wall Street Journal*, January 18, p. 1.

Silk Road Studies Program. 2004. Country Fact Sheets, European Narcotics: Tajikistan 2004. Uppsala University. Online at: http://www.silkroadstudies.org/new/inside/research/narcotics_crime/FactSheet/2004/Tajikistan.pdf (accessed 7/17/07).

Singer, M. 2004. "Why It Is Easier to Get Drugs than Drug Treatment?" In *Unhealthy Health Policy: A Critical Anthropological Examination*, Arachu Castro and Merrill Singer, eds., pp. 287–303. Walnut Creek, CA: Altamira Press.

Singer, M. 2006a. *The Face of Social Suffering: The Life History of a Street Drug Addict*. Long Grove, IL: Waveland Press.

Singer, M. 2006b. *Something Dangerous: Emergent and Changing Illicit Drug Use and Community Health*. Long Grove, IL: Waveland Press.

Singer, M. 2007. *Drugging the Poor: Legal and Illegal Drug Industries and Social Inequality*. Long Grove, IL: Waveland Press.

Singer, M. and Baer, H. 2007. *Introducing Medical Anthropology: A Discipline in Action*. New York: Rowman and Littlefield.

Smith, L. 2006. "Carlos Lehder's Bahamian Legacy." *Bahama Pundit*. Online at: http://www.bahamapundit.com/2006/07/carlos_lehders_.html (accessed 11/3/07).

Soyinka, W. 1996. *The Open Sore of a Continent: A Personal Narrative of the Nigerian Crisis*. New York: Oxford University Press.

Stebbins, K. 1990. "Transnational Tobacco Companies and Health in Underdeveloped Countries: Recommendations for Avoiding a Smoking Epidemic." *Social Science and Medicine* 30:227–235.

Stebbins, K. 2001. "Going Like Gangbusters: Transnational Tobacco Companies 'Making a Killing' in South America." *Medical Anthropology Quarterly* 15:147–170.

Stokes, D. 2005. *America's Other War: Terrorizing Colombia*. London: Zed Books.

Strabroek News. 2006. "Roger Khan, Others Held in Suriname after Drug Bust." June 16. Online at: http://www.stabroeknews.com/index.pl/article_general_news?id=56497389 (accessed 11/20/07).

Strange, S. 1995. "The Defective State." *Daedalus* 124(2) (Spring):55–74.

Straw, W. 1998. The Thingishness of Things. Keynote address for the Interrogating Subcultures Conference, University of Rochester, March 27.

Swartz, B. 2001. "Helping the World Combat International Crime." *Global Issues* 6(2).

Tamayo, J. 2001. "Private Firms Take on U.S. Military Role in Drug War." *Miami Herald*, May 22, p. 1

Thadani, S. 2007. South Asian History: The Colonial Legacy—Myths and Popular Beliefs. Online at: http://india_resource.tripod.com/colonial.html (accessed 12/6/07).

The Times of India. 2001. "Drug Trade in India on a New High." Online at: http://www.poppies.org/2001/09/07/drug-trade-in-india-on-a-new-high (accessed 12/6/07).

The White House. 2003. Joint Statement between the United States of America and the Kingdom of Thailand. Press release, June 11. Online at: http://www.whitehouse.gov/news/releases/2003/06/20030611-1.html (accessed 1/27/08).

Thomas, G. 2005. "Rival Drug Gangs Turn the Streets of Nuevo Laredo into a War Zone." *New York Times*, December 14, p. 5.

Thompson, V. 1968. *French Indochina*. New York: Octagon Books.

Thürer, D. 1999. "The 'Failed State' and International Law." *International Review of the American Red Cross* 836:731–761.

Transnational Institute. 2001. *Merging Wars: Afghanistan, Drugs and Terrorism, Drugs and Conflict Debate*, Paper 3. Amsterdam: Transnational Institute.

Trentlage, B. 2006. "The U.S. War on Drugs: Policy Failure and Strategies for Success." *Modus Vivendi: A Journal of International Affairs* 12:84–109.

UNAIDS. 2004. *Report on the Global AIDS Epidemic*. Geneva, Switzerland: Joint United Nations Programme on HIV/AIDS.

United Nations Department of Economic and Social Affairs. 2006. *The Millennium Development Goals Report*. New York: United Nations.

United Nations Development Programme. 1993. *Human Development Report.* Vienna, Austria: Vienna International Centre.

United Nations Information Service. 2002. Press Release: African Governments Respond to Increasing Illicit Drug Trafficking and Abuse. April 15. Online at: http://www.unis.unvienna.org/unis/pressrels/2002/nar746.html (accessed 9/22/07).

United Nations Information Service. 2004. Press Release: United Nations Counter-Narcotics Chief Visits Central Asia, Urges Regional Cooperation Against Drugs, Crime and Terrorism. May 21. Online at: http://www.un.org/News/Press/docs/2004/socnar904.doc.htm (accessed 7/17/07).

United Nations Office for Drug Control and Crime Prevention. 2003. *Global Illicit Drug Trends, 2003.* United Nations Publication Sales No. E.03.XI.5. Vienna: United Nations.

United Nations Office on Drugs and Crime (UNODC). 1994. *Drugs and Development.* UNDCP Technical Series, No. 1. Vienna, Austria: Vienna International Centre.

United Nations Office on Drugs and Crime (UNODC). 2003. Global Illicit Drug Trends 2003. New York: United Nations Office on Drugs and Crime.

United Nations Office on Drugs and Crime (UNODC). 2006. Drug Abuse and Demand Reduction. Online at: http://www.unodc.org/unodc/en/drug_demand_reduction.html (accessed 1/3/08).

United Nations Office on Drugs and Crime (UNODC). 2007a. UNODC Warns of Cocaine Trafficking Threat in West Africa. Online at: http://www.unodc.org/unodc/en/press/releases/2007-12-12_02.html (accessed 12/20/07).

United Nations Office on Drugs and Crime (UNODC). 2007b. *World Drug Report.* New York: United Nations Office on Drugs and Crime.

U.S. Congress. 1977. Southeast Asian Narcotics. House, Select Committee on Narcotics Abuse and Control Hearings, 95th Congress, 1st Session. Washington, DC: U.S. Government Printing Office.

U.S. Department of State. 2001. Foreign Military Training and DOD Engagement Activities of Interest: Joint Report to Congress for FY 2000-01, Executive Summary. Online at: http://www.state.gov/t/pm/rls/rpt/fmtrpt/2001 (accessed 12/12/07).

U.S. Department of State. 2004. Bush, Uribe Applaud Strength of U.S.–Colombia Partnership. Online at: http://usinfo.state.gov/gi/Archive/2004/Nov/23-231491.html (accessed 12/6/07).

U.S. Department of State. 2007. Guyana. Online at: http://travel.state.gov/travel/cis_pa_tw/cis/cis_1133.html (accessed 4/4/07).

USA Today. 2005. "Jamaica to Hire More Police to Curb High Crime Rate." November 8, p. 11.

Vanichensi, S., Wongsuwan, B., Choopanya, K., and Wongpanich, K. 1991. "A Controlled Trial of Methadone Maintenance in a Population of Intravenous Drug Users in Bangkok: Implications for Prevention of HIV." *International Journal of Addiction* 26(12):1313–1320.

Vásquez, I. 2002. "The International War on Drugs." In *Cato Handbook for Congress: Policy Recommendations for the 108th Congress,* pp. 567–576. Washington, DC: The Cato Institute.

Wallerstein, I. 1979. *The Capitalist World-System: Essays*. New York: Cambridge University Press.

Wallerstein, I. 1994. "Lodestar or Illusion." In *Capitalism and Development, Immanuel Wallerstein and Development Studies*, Leslie Sklair, ed., pp. 3–20. London: Routledge.

Wallis-Wells, B. 2007. "How America Lost the War on Drugs." *Rolling Stone*. Online at: http://www.rollingstone.com/news/story/174388397/how_America_lost_the_war_on_drugs (accessed 11/20/06).

Waters, W. 2001. "Globalization, Socioeconomic Restructuring, and Community Health." *Journal of Community Health* 26(2):79–92.

Wilkinson, B. 2006. Guyana: Weary of Drugs and Crime, Some Voters Eye New Party. Inter Press Service News Agency. Online at: http://www.ipsnews.net/news.asp?idnews=34468 (accessed 4/4/06).

Windstone, S. 2002. Nigeria: A Country in Search of Nationhood. Online at: http://www.inch.com/~shebar/nigeria/nation1.htm (accessed 12/7/07).

Wolf, E. 1982. *Europe and the People without History*. Berkeley: University of California Press.

World Bank. 1993. *World Development Report 1993: Investing in Health*. Washington, DC: Oxford University Press.

Worldpress.org. 2007. Guinea-Bissau: Fears of an Emerging Narco-State. Online at: http://www.worldpress.org/Africa/2660.cfm (accessed 12/2/07).

Yongming, Z. 1997. *Anti-Drug Crusades in Twentieth Century China: Nationalism, History and State Building*. Lanham, MD: Rowman and Littlefield.

Youngers, C. and Rosin, E. 2004. "The U.S. 'War on Drugs': Its Impact on Latin America and the Caribbean." In *Drugs and Democracy in Latin America: The Impact of U.S. Policy*, Coletta Youngers and Eileen Rosin, eds., pp. 1–14. Boulder, CO: Lynne Rienner.

Zamorano, J. 2007. Panama Declares U.S. Invasion Date a National Day of Mourning. MSNBC Wire Services. Online at: http://www.msnbc.msn.com/id/22346734 (accessed 12/20/07).

Zill, O. and Bergman, L. 2001. "U.S. Business and Money Laundering." *FRONTLINE*. Online at: www.pbs.org/wgbh/pages/frontline/shows/drugs/special/us.html (accessed 3/4/06).

Zill, O. 2002. International Smuggling Overview. April 19. Transcript online at: http://www.pbs.org/now/politics/smuggling.html (accessed 11/22/07).

Index